THE EQUINE ARENA HANDBOOK

DEVELOPING A USER-FRIENDLY FACILITY

Robert Malmgren

"Good footing is no accident, but poor footing is."

The Equine Arena Handbook
Developing a User-Friendly Facility

Library of Congress Cataloging-in-Publication Data

Malmgren, Robert C.
The equine arena handbook: developing a user-friendly facility / Robert Malmgren.
p. cm.
Includes bibliographical references (p.).
ISBN 1-57779-016-2
1. Horse arenas--Design and construction. I. Title.
SF294.35.M35 1999
725'.82--dc21
99-26226
CIP

This book is available at special quantity discounts for clubs for promotions, premiums, or educational use. Write for details.

Editor: Deborah Helmers
Cover & Text Design: Tammy Geiger, M.S.
Cover photos:
Background, Robert Malmgren
Reining horse, © Ollie Griffith
Dressage horse, Stephen Bradley on Delta Deuce © Dusty Perin

4 5 6 7 8 9 0

PRINTED IN THE UNITED STATES OF AMERICA

Dedicated to
the six million horses in the United States
and their care-givers
who stand to be the recipients of user-friendly footing.

Acknowledgments

Deep appreciation is extended to those who have so generously helped in the preparation of this handbook. Dr. Ed Umlauf, a veterinarian in the Denver area, strongly emphasized the need for research on footing materials based upon injuries documented in the racetrack industry. The three contrasting arena facilities at Colorado State University provided an opportunity to study ranges in footing types and intensity of use. The high level of participation by Kevin Hodges, Research Assistant, is much appreciated. The encouragement, suggestions and questions posed by Dr. R. K. Shideler and the willingness of Dr. Wayne McIlwraith (director, Equine Teaching and Research Center, CSU) to explore new methods are acknowledged by the author. Valued for their openness in expressing their opinions regarding footing evaluations and certain management practices are Heather Schoning, Instructor, Ann Westhoff, and Ron Olinger. Finally, Mary Grace Coming took on the typing of the manuscript.

Contents

Preface

Equine facilities throughout the world, whether racetracks or arenas, show wide variations in construction and maintenance which often are reflected in wide ranges in performance. Commonly, performance has been credited to or blamed on the horse. Mary Bromiley, a horse trainer/physiotherapist in England, made this statement to the author: "Consistency [of the footing] is one of the keys to performance of the equine athlete and this is true whether you are talking about Thoroughbred racing, jumping, or barrel-racing."

Consistency involves traction, resiliency/hardness, and moisture content. These qualities represent the "effect" part of the equation, if you will. The "cause" side of the equation consists of a number of soil parameters: particle-size distribution (texture), mineralogy (e.g., quartz, feldspar, etc.), water-holding capacity, and drainage. In addition, weather for outdoor facilities can play an important role in the condition of the footing, enhancing or degrading its consistency.

Managing your facility is thus clearly more than a decision to replace the footing or to add "something" to it. Rather, it involves a holistic approach to understanding exactly what you have and how well you can expect it to perform with optimum management of the arena.

The equine athlete has received his share of injuries over the years, but only recently have studies revealed a relationship between footing condition and the incidence of certain types of injuries.[1] While this does not rule out genetic factors and the condition of the horse in question, footing cannot be ignored. This appears to be a factor on arena facilities as well as on racetracks, where considerable research has been carried out.

In 1987, the author was given the opportunity to evaluate what effect, if any, crumb rubber might have on the round pens at the CSU Equine Center in Fort Collins, Colorado. These two pens, forty feet and sixty feet in diameter, were not used on a regular basis, but when used they were used heavily. They had been constructed with six inches of construction grade sand overlying a base designed as a roadbed. The problem with both pens was one of hardness, and, related to that problem, drainage. Because they were outdoor facilities, they were subject to the whims of Colorado's weather—rain, snow, wind, and extremes in temperature. The fifteen percent crumb rubber added to the sand in one round pen provided a substantially more resilient surface and greatly improved the drainage compared to the control pen, which had no rubber mixed in.

Footing resiliency is not the only area of concern. In 1991, while carrying out a hardness evaluation in the main arena at CSU, Dr. Robert Shideler became interested in the device I was using to test hardness (the Clegg Impact Tester). He remarked, "I understand the significance of what you're doing with regard to hardness, but I think the problem of dust is equally important and more readily recognized. In fact, some days the telephone nearly rings off the hook with individuals seeking an answer to dust problems."

Research has been ongoing by the author since 1989, as well as prior to his work at CSU. Much has been learned and consequently much can be shared with others—hence this handbook.

If there is any one fact learned during this ongoing study, it is that there is no single recipe for getting on top of the problems of *dust, hardness, drainage,* and *performance*. These four issues are interrelated, and consequently a holistic approach must be taken to better understand their treatment.

The starting point in resolving any arena difficulty is to determine, in detail, the composition of the footing in that particular arena. A lab analysis of composition usually includes, at a minimum, particle-size distribution, sand size, and percentage of organic matter. By themselves, terms like *dirt* or *sand* are meaningless. When you know exactly what you are dealing with regarding your footing, the decision becomes easier as to whether you keep it, modify it, or start over. Understanding the composition of your footing will also enable you to be more effective in working and watering your arena.

While research has been funded in the United States as well as other countries in an attempt to find the answers to racetrack breakdown, very little work has been carried out—or at least published—with regard to the challenges of equine arenas. The racing industry's prime focus is related to hardness, drainage, and thickness of cushion and their possible role in injury to the equine athlete. The type and intensity of use in arenas is quite different.

This book is designed to bring to light how construction details and maintenance can influence the performance of the arena and, ultimately, the performance and health of the equine athlete. The relationship between arena condition and arena performance has not always been fully appreciated. Some of the problems involve the wide range of the materials collectively called *dirt*. Different materials respond differently to watering and working and can produce a footing differing widely in performance. Construction details and the use and management of the arena all determine to what degree you can achieve a high performance arena.

The future for the arena manager will involve an increasing emphasis on construction and maintenance details that enhance performance by developing a reasonably consistent surface and base for the event. In addition, focus will be on minimizing the dust potential of the footing to reduce the incidence of related health problems to the equine athlete. Along with this last point will come an increased awareness of the most effective use of water on the arena. Finally, discerning the best use of manure from an equine facility will be key as the number of horses continues to grow along with the number of humans on our planet. Concerns over water and air quality and fly control will only grow—the days of the manure pile, as such, are limited. With most landfills unable to accept manure, composting becomes a logical alternative.

Hopefully, this handbook will shed some light on these challenges. While it is one of the first books on this general subject, it is hoped it will stimulate interest in furthering research in the important field of equine arenas.

1. Cheney, J. A., Shen, C. K., Wheat, J. D. "Relationship of racetrack surface to lameness in the the Thoroughbred racehorse," *American Journal of Veterinary Research* 34 (10) (1973): 1285-1289;
Hill, T., Maylin, G., Krook, L. "Track condition and racing injuries in Thoroughbred horses," *Cornell Veterinarian* 76 (1986): 361-379;
Moyer, W., Spencer, P. A., Kallish, M. "Relative incidence of dorsal metacarpal disease in young Thoroughbred racing horses training on two surfaces," *Equine Veterinary Journal* 23 (3) (1990): 166-168;
Sellnow, L. "The science of safety," *Blood-Horse,* September 1991;
Zebarth, B. J., Sheard, R. W. "Impact and shear resistance of turf grass racing surfaces for Thoroughbreds," *American Journal of Veterinary Research* 46 (4) (1985): 778-786.

1

Soil Essentials

FUNDAMENTALS

Any book discussing equine arenas would fall short of its goal if a description of the mantle covering the surface of the earth (soil) were not included. Either directly or indirectly, soils or soil materials are related to the quality of an equine facility. Soils, by definition, are comprised of mineral and organic matter with varying amounts of air and water in them. The air and water move through the soils via pores which vary in size from very fine (not visible to the naked eye) to coarse (readily observed without the aid of magnification). The largest individual use made of soils is in the production of plants, including forests, pastures, orchards, and row crops.

In the United States alone there are over 10,000 different soils. Each of these soils has been identified with a name (such as *Colby Silt Loam,* for example) and has certain characteristics which determine its capability for certain uses. Some soils are more productive than others. Many have inherent chemical and/or physical problems; quite often these can be modified once the specific problem is identified. Soils come in all colors—black, grey, yellow, brown, and red—with a multitude of different shades or intensities of each color possible.

In addition to their agronomic, horticultural and forestry uses, soils have long been used for roads, airstrips, the foundation for buildings, golf courses, athletic facilities, and, increasingly, for equine facilities, including arenas and racetracks. In the same way that not all soils are well adapted for the growth of apples or cotton, so also not all soils are appropriate for an equine facility. When it comes to equine facilities, we have two concerns: First, how suitable is the on-site soil material for a sub-base and, in some cases, for the base; and second, how suitable is the material for use as footing? In most cases, it will be necessary to go beyond a visual test and proceed to a few simple tests that can be run by most soil labs. Even though the sub-base may start at ten to twenty inches below the surface of the arena, its suitability must be determined in advance. The right materials for the footing, base and sub-base will ensure the potential for optimum performance and long life for the facility. With poorly suited material, arena maintenance becomes difficult, performance variable, and the potential for re-doing the arena highly possible.

PROBLEMS WITH POORLY SUITED MATERIALS

What are some of the characteristics of poorly suited materials?

Footing

Dust

- A result of a high percent of fine and very fine sand, plus silt.
- Very low water-holding capacity.
- Water-repellent soil.

Hardness

- Certain soil textures compact easily with sandy loam, rating high for hardness potential and creating a hazard for the equine athlete.
- A quick test for determining the hardness potential is to take about a heaping tablespoon of the soil in question, moisten it to the point of saturation, roll it between the thumb and index finger to the diameter of a coarse wire (l/8-l/4 inch diameter), allow to dry and determine its relative hardness.

Base/Sub-base

- Certain subsoils found in the high rainfall zones of Hawaii are "smeary," or slick, when moist and are unstable for supporting the arena.
- Many soils in Colorado, Nebraska, and Wyoming have a high shrink-swell potential. When they are wet, they expand; when dry, they crack. This situation provides very poor support for arenas as well as for building construction.

SOURCES OF ASSISTANCE

- The Soil Survey Report for your particular county provides a quick, in-depth look at the soils on your property.
- The personnel at the Natural Resources Conservation office (formerly called Soil Conservation Service) might also yield some helpful information on your soils.
- Work with an arena consultant.
- Work with a soil-testing lab.

ADDITIONAL ON-SITE CONCERNS

Other soil-related phenomena include: frost action, run-on, run-off, salt-affected soils, and clods.

Frost Action

Soils subject to frost action resulting in frost heaving are of particular concern to outdoor arenas in temperate climates. Problem areas include not only the northern states, but also the high elevation areas of the western states. Frost heaving can fracture a base and, over time, can bring gravel and stones to the surface. Because they frequently have gravelly/stony subsoils, mountain soils in particular are subject to gravel and stones thrust up to the surface. Those soils with a higher silt content have a higher potential for frost heave.

This "dirt" arena built over a base of road-bed material has a significant amount of gravel and cobbles on the surface. These coarse fragments appear to increase in number due to frost heaving.

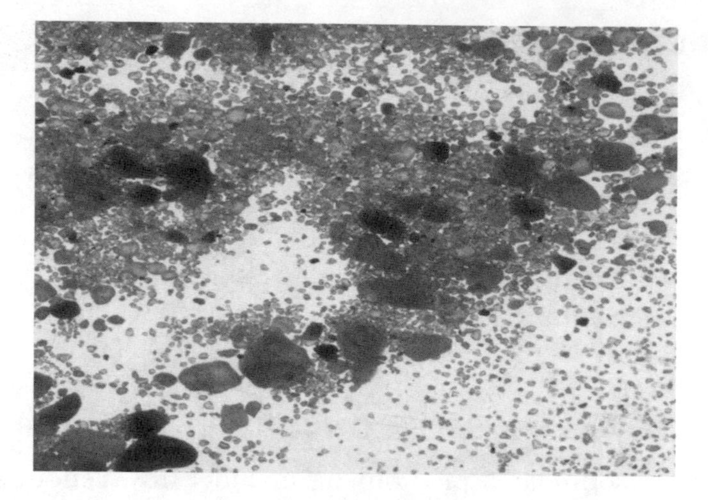

This photo shows the variable sizes of sand particles in one kind of sand bought from a supplier.

Run-on

If your arena is located in a lower position than the surrounding area, it could be subject to periodic coverage with water from the surrounding slopes. Flood plain locations should be avoided. These can be fairly well identified based on their position and soil type; often they are supporting wet-land vegetation.

Run-off

When water accumulates on an outdoor arena with a definite slope of greater than one percent, it will run off, creating rills where the footing has been removed.

Salt-affected Soils

Salt-affected soils are found mostly in the arid and semiarid zones of the United States. In addition, U.S. coastal areas are frequently salt-affected. Wherever these soils are found, drainage, water movement into the soil, dust management, and general performance may be challenging.

Clods

When soils having a particular combination of silt and clay content are subjected to compaction followed by the use of certain tillage equipment, the result is a surface littered with irregular clumps of soil known as *clods,* which range in size up to ten inches in diameter. Clods are more apt to be formed when the moisture content is too high for a dirt arena to be worked.

VARIABILITY OF SOILS

Soils can and do change quite abruptly within a short distance. For this reason, the site that you have selected for your arena needs to be sampled on a grid basis, with samples observed to a depth of at least eighteen inches, to be sure you have essentially the same soil material throughout. Sample spacing can be made every seven to ten feet. This will pick up any contrasting conditions regarding texture and drainage, which will determine whether the site is suitable or you need to look for another. In some cases, the Soil Survey Report will be in sufficient detail, giving one designated soil type on your property. You can then read the characteristics and qualities of the soil in question. While the report will not rate the soil for suitability for arenas, a soil rated as Class I for cropland could be very well suited for an arena. Your county Natural Resources Conservation person might work with you on this decision.

ADDITIONAL COMMENTS

Soil was one of the first building materials used by mankind. Primitive man built his shelters in and on this readily available material. In fact, the most common building materials in parts of Africa and Asia today are certain types of soil. The problem with soil as a building material, whether for an arena in the United States or a family home in the tropics, is in its lack of uniformity. Soils have varied origins (differences in parent materials) and are likely to be of a very heterogeneous composition. For this reason, soil-sampling techniques and testing procedures can do much to eliminate the guesswork and resultant disappointment.

The following are points to consider:

- Soils don't just happen; they have a certain composition and behavior depending on the material(s) from which they were formed.

- Most soils vary considerably with increasing depth, with the better soil material being near or at the surface. With increasing depth, the soil usually becomes less desirable for footing due to the higher clay content, but it may be suitable for a base.
- Improving the condition of soil materials by the addition of another material is called *soil modification*. For example, sand may be added to loosen up a tight clay soil. Depending on the degree of change needed and the cost and availability of the material to be added, this may or may not be cost-effective.
- Most mapped soils will be labeled as to drainage class. This implies, among other things, the depth to a water table and whether or not the downward movement of water is slow or rapid. "Well drained" and "very well drained" are the best drainage classes for most arena or track facilities.
- A condition known as *dry consistence* is an important clue for predicting how the soil will perform as a footing. To test for dry consistence, take a tablespoon of soil, moisten it, press it between your thumb and index finger, roll it into a ball and let it dry. If it doesn't adhere but falls apart, there is no problem. If it forms a "ribbon" when pressed between your thumb and index finger and dries hard when in a ball, this is less than desirable material for footing. Chances are it will be dusty, hard, and difficult to work up without several equipment passes.
- Some soils in the arid parts of the world have a high salt content and may hold onto any water very tenaciously. When used for arena construction, such soils result in generally poor conditions being the rule rather than the exception.

2

Arena Floor Basics

THE FOOTING

The most obvious part of any arena floor is the surface or the footing material. Whether it is natural (sand or dirt), organic (shavings, sawdust), recycled materials such as crumb rubber (1/8-3/8 inch rubber particles derived from shredding used tires), or some combination of these materials, it will be subject to certain demands. The least obvious trait of any surface is the extent to which it will be "user-friendly" for the equine athlete. In addition, will its maintenance requirements be reasonable or excessive?

In order to anticipate reasonable satisfaction from your surface, the material(s) comprising it should meet your particular objectives with regard to the type and intensity of use you intend. In addition, these materials should have inherent qualities of low dust potential (see Chapter 7) and a low potential for hardness (see Chapter 9).

A number of factors will help you determine the type of surface to choose. Among these are budget, the availability of local materials, specific objectives, your soil quality on-site, your priorities, your equipment for working the arena, and your water supply, including cost. If you decide to use the material already there (the soil on-site), you may want or need to add a footing amendment to improve it. One example of a footing amendment is a crumb rubber addition to a sand or dirt surface (see Chapter 13). The addition of crumb rubber, however, should only be made if the existing surface material is not degraded to a level of "poor" condition. This is the point of no return with regard to attempting to improve the footing with an addition. If the condition is "poor," the best alternative is to remove the old footing, and then add a quality sand plus crumb rubber. However, good footing alone is not enough to ensure good performance—a well-designed base and sub-base are crucial for an arena.

The arena's footing is essential for a good performance by horse and rider. Tammy Geiger and Mr. Scat Bar. Photo by Dalco Photography.

THE BASE

The base of the arena is a protective and supportive "cap." It should be made from uniform material that can be compacted so as to be nearly impenetrable. This provides a consistent or uniform subsurface immediately below the footing. With this type of base and periodic checking on its competency, there is little chance of letting your horse down.

Broadly speaking, there are three categories of base construction. One of the more common techniques is to remove the topsoil, grade with either a crown or a slant, and then add your footing. The reason for the removal of the topsoil is that most topsoil material is more friable than desired and has sufficient organic matter in it so as to limit its compactability. In some parts of the country, the subsoil remaining after topsoil removal is "terra firma" in every sense of those words; in other areas, it will need to be rolled before applying the footing; and in some cases you may find soil material which is not too different from the sand you may have chosen for your footing. Assuming you did your exploratory work prior to bringing in the construction equipment, the next step in this last scenario would be to bring in a suitable material with enough silt and clay to be mixed with the subsoil, allowing it to be firmed up after rolling.

A second, more advanced base construction involves the use of a single layer of aggregate base material following the removal of the topsoil and grading of the area. Materials used for this purpose are commonly referred to as *screenings* and contain rock fragments up to one-half inch and finer particles down to silt and clay in size. The finer particles provide for the material to be firm after rolling when moist. The availability of base material can vary with the part of the country in which you live. The rock type may be basalt, bluestone granite, or in some areas, asphalt. This then is compacted with a heavy—preferably a twenty-ton—roller. If recycled asphalt is used (the salvaged material when an asphalt road is being replaced) an additive should be used to optimize cohesiveness of the asphalt material. Without the additive the asphalt will break apart even with the use of a vibrating roller. At the present time there are no standards regarding the composition of recycled asphalt. Sand, gravel and actual asphalt can vary considerably.

The third type of base construction involves an increase in sophistication, as well as in price. Through the use of material such as an aggregate base or, in some cases, a drainage aggregate along with geotextile fabric and stone dust, the quality of the facility improves. However, the higher the investment, the greater the need for a high level of maintenance.

The type of construction used should be based on your particular site requirements. For outdoor arenas, climate is a critical factor. Precipitation, temperature, snow cover and freeze-thaw action, with its potential for frost heaving, need to be considered.

In outdoor arenas, the tendency often is "to use the ground that's there because it is hard anyway." If you are considering buying horse property with an outdoor arena, the presence of weeds in the arena is an indication that the base was not heavily packed and is still a suitable medium for plant growth. Most soils, other than peat and straight sand, will appear hard at times as you try to work them or even just walk over them. Most soils are at their hardest when they are dry; just how hard will depend on the clay type and the amount of

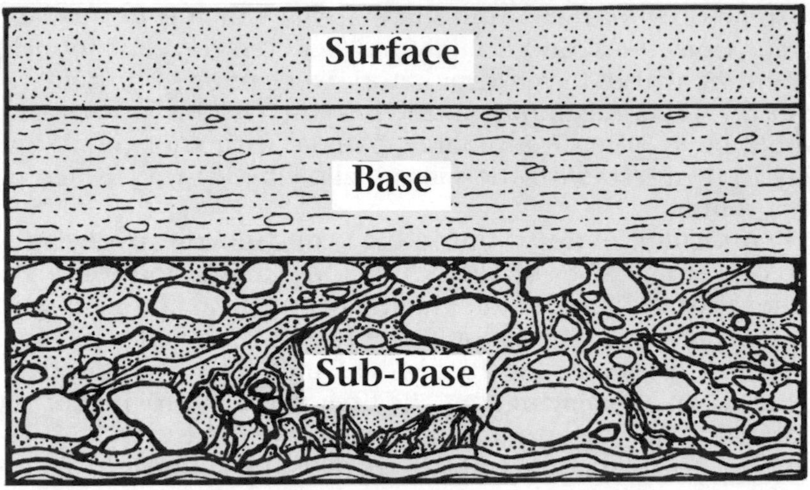

Schematic diagram showing the position of the components of a designed arena floor. The thickness of surface and base can vary depending on the dominant type of events held on the facility. Each of these three components has a specific function; these can best be enhanced by specifying the materials to be used for the surface and the base. The sub-base is the material already existing on the site. Good site selection is, therefore, critical for the performance and life of the arena.

silt, clay, and organic matter. Whether or not your soil is suitable for base material can best be determined by sampling in the laboratory.

How to Sample

A lab result is only as accurate as the sampling procedure. It is important to know what you are gathering for your representative sample soil and that it truly represents a soil type that has the best potential for base construction. This is usually subsoil material, free of sandy material, gravel and organic matter, including roots. The analysis to request is particle-size distribution showing the percent of sand, silt, and clay present. The laboratory doing the analysis in your area should be able to tell you if this material has the potential to be hard when compacted and, in general, to serve as a base for your arena.

Consequences of a Poorly Planned Base

Without a distinct base in an arena facility, the "bottom" would be variable in depth, hardness, drainage, rock or gravel content, and ultimately, performance. The changes that occur in a sand footing have two major causes. The first is abrasion, discussed in the next chapter. The second is the mixing of the base soil with the footing. The increased silt and clay added from the base will change the texture, the water handling, and the performance of the footing and its management requirements.

The odds of a footing enhancer (rubber or wood fiber, e.g.) benefiting an arena are substantially reduced when the basics have not been satisfactorily assessed and dealt with. No one wins in this situation. The salespeople lose credibility, the owners of the facility make a poor investment, and the users still aren't happy. The old adage that a chain is no stronger than its weakest link still holds—a poor base will undermine even the most expensive footing.

The arena footing must be able to absorb a very large amount of the impact when the horse makes contact with the surface, and still be firm enough to support take-off points as well. Photo by Dusty Perin.

THE SUB-BASE

The sub-base is the foundation of the arena facility. It is the layer of material below the base, and is almost always found on-site. It must be well-drained and stable. To determine the suitability of soil for the sub-base, check the soils map for your property, which will give you information on texture and drainage and other necessary data. Soils rated suitable for agriculture could be acceptable for your purposes also.

ADDITIONAL COMMENTS

The arena floor is that portion of an arena that receives traffic. Ideally it should be designed and constructed to offer a surface yielding optimum performance of the equine athlete with a reasonable level of maintenance. The lowest bid on materials or construction of an arena may or may not be your best bet. As you would with any other contractor, ask for references regarding similar facilities he or she has built. Be sure the materials to be used will contribute to the quality of the facility. Tests should be made on those materials that have been selected for the base and the footing to ensure their suitability. Unsuitable materials and questionable construction can lead to extra maintenance problems and excessive costs, to say nothing about poor performance of or possible injury to the equine athlete.

3

Sand

DEFINITION

The word *arena* means *sand* in Latin. It was the practice in Rome to spread sand on the floor of the stadium to absorb the blood resulting from combat with beasts or between gladiators. What exactly is this substance called *sand*?

Sand, by definition, is an accumulation of tiny pieces of rocks or minerals that are larger than silt or clay but smaller than gravel. (See Table 1 for specific size limits.) Most sands started out as components of larger rocks which over time have been "worn down" by the action of wind, water, and glaciers known as physical weathering. In many areas the only sand available is from crushed rock.

Sands vary considerably because of their mineral composition, how they were formed, their range in particle size and shape of the sand grains, and the type and amount of so-called impurities in the sand. The dominant mineral in most sands is quartz, but sand may also include other minerals such as feldspar, mica, magnetite, ilmenite and zircon.

Some natural sand deposits are composed of minerals other than quartz; examples are the gypsum sands of the White Sands National Monument in New Mexico, the olivene sand found in limited quantity on certain Hawaiian beaches, the calcite (coral) sands of the Bermuda beaches, and the black sands found in Hawaii, consisting of grains of basalt and basaltic glass.

How a sand was formed will dictate the shape of the individual sand grains. Material that has been rolled and tossed by wave action along a beach will tend to be predominantly rounded, while rock material that has been crushed without being transported too far—for example, by the action of plant roots and a freeze-thaw action—will tend to have more angular-shaped grains.

MINERALOGY OF SANDS

All natural sands have been developed from the dominant rocks or minerals of the region where they were formed. Many sands are principally formed from the mineral quartz and are relatively hard compared with sands formed from micas such as biotite and muscovite.

SHAPE OF SAND GRAINS

Sand particles vary in shape from angular to rounded to sub-angular or sub-rounded. All shapes may be found in one sand sample. Sands to avoid are those that are dominantly rounded, as these create a "soft" sand, and those of the other extreme, the angular, which can create a "hard" sand. In addition to the shape of the sand grains, size distribution and surface roughness also affect the packing and compressibility of sands.

SIZE OF SAND PARTICLES

Some sands are dominated by one or two sizes while others contain the full spectrum of sizes permitted by the definition of sand. Briefly, sands are defined by their particle sizes and include rock or mineral fragments ranging in size from 2.0 mm to 0.05 mm.

Arenas are usually used for a wide variety of activities, and arena requirements for each activity should be taken into consideration. Rodeo events also require an excellent footing for optimum performances.

Table 1.
Sand Separate Classes Compared to Silt and Clay.*

SEPARATE	PARTICLE DIAMETER (mm)	NUMBER OF PARTICLES (per gram)
Sand		
Very coarse sand	2.00 - 1.00	90
Coarse sand	1.00 - 0.50	720
Medium sand	0.50 - 0.25	5,700
Fine sand	0.25 - 0.10	46,000
Very fine sand	0.10 - 0.05	722,000
Silt	0.05 - 0.002	5,776,000
Clay	Below 0.002	90,260,853,000

*The five sand fractions are all visible to the naked eye. Silt particles are visible with the aid of a microscope while clay particles require an electron microscope to be seen.

If you purchase washed sand from your supplier, most of the "impurities" of the natural sand will be removed. Examples of such "impure" materials are silt, clay and, sometimes, organic matter.

While sand is a preferred material for arena footings, its potential variability (in size, shape, hardness, and mineral composition) is wide, and this is one reason for the mixed results people experience when comparing sands in different parts of the country. In Hawaii, the golf course industry purchases sand from Australia for the construction of sand-based greens. This is because Hawaii, even though surrounded by sand, has sands derived predominantly from coral and shells and comprised mostly of rounded grains due to the rolling action of the ocean.

These sands are not well suited for golf-green construction or arena footings. (An additional reason for Hawaii to import sand is that few, if any, natural sand deposits occur in Hawaii and there is a need to protect the esthetics of the beach areas rather than exploit them.)

Sandy soils are used on arena surfaces as well as other high-traffic facilities because they possess better physical properties to accommodate heavy traffic than those soils with an appreciable silt and clay content. It should be kept in mind, however, that sandy soils vary considerably in their physical properties, and, consequently, certain problems can arise due to those properties.

In the U.S.D.A. classification of soils, the three texture classes with the highest content of sand are sand, loamy sand, and sandy loam (see Table 2). As we have seen, sand separates are defined by diameter of the particles. When two soils are classified as sands but one is primarily comprised of the larger diameter very coarse and coarse sands, while the other is dominated by the medium, fine, and very fine sands, the physical properties of the two soils can vary considerably. Moisture retention is but one such variable property, with the finer sands holding somewhat more moisture.

Table 2.
Sand, Silt and Clay Contents of Sandy Soils.*

	Composition percent by weight		
Texture Class	Sand	Silt	Clay
Sand	85 - 100	0 - 15	0 - 15
Loamy sand	70 - 90	0 - 30	10 - 30
Sandy loam	45 - 85	0 - 50	15 - 55

*All particle-size information taken from "Soil Taxonomy, a Basic System of Soil Classification for Making and Interpreting Soil Surveys," *U.S.D.A. Agricultural Handbook* No. 436 (1975).

PARTICLE-SIZE DISTRIBUTION

Sands with a wide particle-size distribution are harder because the particles fit together into a more dense matrix.

Soft sands occur when the sand particles are round and in a narrow particle-size range. The end result is that the surface shifts easily, exhibiting a very weak shear strength. Hence, those sands that are too uniform, that is, that are comprised predominantly of one or two particle sizes, should be avoided. Control measures to correct soft sand after it has been diagnosed include adding organic matter in the form of a high grade of compost and maintaining good moisture levels during periods of use. Care should be taken to obtain a *moist* moisture level, *not wet, not dry.*

SAND PERFORMANCE

There are several ways that sands differ. As indicated earlier, to label a mineral material *sand* means it has a range in particle size from 0.05 mm to 2.00 mm. Particles smaller than very fine sand are termed *silt* or *clay*; particles larger than very coarse sand are called *gravel*. A grab sample of sand, whether it is a natural deposit or made from crushed rock, will show a wide range in particle sizes. If you specify a particular type of sand, such as *masonry sand*, the material will have passed through certain sieves and will have a narrower range in particle size than, say, construction or fill sand.

Sands of different grain size perform differently in an arena. The more fine and very fine particle sizes in a sand, the greater the dust potential. In addition to particle size, the particular mineral composition of the sand grains will determine its "hardness" and its wearing quality before it becomes airborne as dust. While many sands are dominated by quartz, some sands have a significant amount of softer minerals which wear down faster, ultimately producing dust.

From the standpoint of performance, the matter of particle *shape* also is of importance. Dominantly rounded or subrounded particles have a high potential to roll and are consequently less stable than angular or sub-angular grains.

One of the main reasons for variability in performance of

sands lies in the failure to recognize the physical differences between materials that qualify as sands. Four sub-categories have been defined within the general category of sand:

- *Coarse sand*: 25 percent or more very coarse and coarse sand and less than 50 percent any other one grade of sand.
- *Sand*: 25 percent or more very coarse, coarse, and medium sand and less than 50 percent fine or very fine sand.
- *Fine sand*: 50 percent or more fine sand, less than 25 percent very coarse, coarse, and medium sand and less than 50 percent very fine sand.
- *Very fine sand*: 50 percent or more very fine sand.

The difference between coarse sand and very fine sand is readily apparent to most people, but distinguishing between sand and fine sand is somewhat more difficult. The important differences, however, go beyond appearance. The sands also perform differently and require different management with regard to hardness and dust. The potential for dust and hardness increases as the percentage of fine and very fine sands increases. Strength also increases with an increase in fine sand compared with coarse sand. This latter point becomes critical when it comes to the take-off for horse jumping.

BUYING SAND

Those involved in the sale of sand use general names for the different types of sand available. Common general names include:

- *Concrete sand*—usually contains a wide particle-size range of sands and fine gravel.
- *Masonry sand*—similar to concrete sand but without the fine gravel.
- *Structural fill*—less than one-quarter inch chip and sand mix.
- *River sand*—quite variable with regard to the amount of fines (silt and clay) contained. These finer materials tend to increase the dust potential.
- *Washed sands*—Washing tends to remove silt and clay from the sand.

Depending on your geographical area, other types of sand may be available locally, for example, *dune sand*. These sands will need a lab analysis to determine their particle-size range before using.

WEIGHT AND VOLUME OF SAND

Most often sand is sold on a weight basis, in tons. If you are thinking in terms of cubic yards, remember that a cubic foot of dry sand weighs about 100 pounds. Since there are 27 cubic feet per cubic yard, one cubic yard of sand weighs about 2,700 pounds. If you divide 2,700 pounds by 2,000 pounds, you get the figure of 1.35. Therefore, to convert yards to tons, multiply the number of cubic yards by 1.35.

How much sand is required for your arena? Again, assuming one cubic foot of sand weighs 100 pounds, the following weights are a pretty good guideline:

2.0" of sand = 16.66 lb./sq.ft.
3.0" of sand = 25.0 lb./sq.ft.
4.0" of sand = 33.33 lb./sq.ft.

Multiply the number of square feet in your arena by the weight for the selected thickness and you'll have the total number of pounds needed. Convert to tons by dividing by 2,000.

DO SANDS WEAR OUT?

Sands do wear out over time. The rate that this happens varies with the mineralogy of the sand (with quartz grains being most durable), the intensity of use of the arena, and arena maintenance. Dry sands and footings that have become thin are more subject to the effects of abrasion than moist sands and footings of an optimum depth. Studies at CSU showed a marked sand degradation after six months of light to moderate use on an indoor arena 80 by 180 feet in size. The sieve analysis of the sand after this period of time showed a large decrease in the very coarse sand, a moderate decrease in the coarse sand, and a substantial increase in the moderate, fine, and very fine sand. Remember that fine and very fine sands contribute to the dust hazard potential.

New sand as seen with an electron microscope, showing angular sand grains with a size range of very coarse, medium, and fine grains. This is from a sample of washed concrete sand prior to use in an arena. This material has a low dust potential.

The same sand after six months' use as footing. The grain size is smaller, with medium grains dominating, and with few coarse and many fine and very fine sand grains. Most of the grains are somewhat rounded due to abrasion. The dust potential is now higher.
Micrographs by Dr. John Chandler, Electron Microscopy Center, Colorado State University.

SANDS WITH SILT AND CLAY CONTENT

After sand, the next major category of coarse-textured soils is the loamy sands. Loamy sands are soil materials that contain at the upper limit eighty-five to ninety percent sand with a total silt and clay content of not less than fifteen percent.

The important difference between the sands and loamy sands is that the latter contains a higher percentage of silt and clay. Loamy sands, for this reason, have a higher moisture retention capability, but they also have a higher dust potential.

Sandy loam is less common than either sand or loamy sand because it cannot readily or easily be "manufactured" as can sand by the crushing of rocks. This texture contains increasingly higher percentages of silt and clay than loamy sands. The sandy loam texture is therefore highly susceptible to soil compaction.

WATER-HOLDING CAPACITY OF SANDS AND OTHER SOIL MATERIALS

In the process of applying water to reduce the dust problem of an arena, we need to consider the type of material (soil texture) as well as the condition of the material. Soil textures differ in the amount of water they will hold. Table 3 shows that the amount of water a soil will hold varies considerably as you go from coarse-textured materials to medium- and fine-textured ones.

Table 3.
Influence of Soil Type on Water-Holding Capacity.

SOIL TYPE	TOTAL WATER-HOLDING CAPACITY (inches of water held per foot of soil)
Sand—coarse textured	0.6 - 1.8
Loam—medium textured	2.7 - 4.0
Clay—fine textured	4.5 - 4.9

The above figures are intended as a guide for how much water to apply to your arena. If you have an arena with 4.0 inches of coarse sand on the surface and you used the lower figure of 0.6 inch per one foot of soil, you then would apply a maximum of 0.2 inches of water if you were starting with a dry surface. The factor of *condition* comes into the picture in determining how well the very coarse sand material handles this amount of water, including the rate at which it may be applied to the surface without flooding or run-off. Water applied faster than the soil can absorb it will create puddling or run-off. Similarly, water applied in excess of storage capacity may create wet and/or slippery areas on the surface, with excess water pene-

A problem that arises when sands wear out—dust. Chad Griess on Paint. Photo by Tammy Geiger.

trating the base, thereby losing the uniformity of the base. Both create footing problems. This waste of water can be costly where water rates or pumping costs are high. In areas where water is scarce, avoiding over-watering is critical. (Please see Chapter 8.)

ADDITIONAL COMMENTS

Sand is a specific material with a specific range in grain size. Not uncommonly, material from a creek bank has been used for footing only to find out it requires high maintenance to keep it loose and provide drainage.

Construction grade sand may appear like pretty decent material, but it is not washed and contains appreciable levels of silt and clay. This ultimately leads to dust problems and a footing subject to hardening after use and, particularly, after drying out.

4

Dirt

TERMINOLOGY

When mineral material other than sand is used for footing, it is usually a soil material comprised of sand, silt, and clay, plus organic material. The sand content is by definition less than eighty-five percent as determined by a mechanical analysis in a soil lab. We call this mineral material *dirt*.

Dirt, as it pertains to equine arenas and as used in this handbook, is a collective term covering a wide range of materials used as footing. Sand differs from dirt in being a coarser-grained material.

A dirt footing functions differently from a sand one in the following ways:

- Dirt is not as free-draining as sand.
- Dirt requires more tractor power to work.
- Dirt has a higher potential water-holding capacity than sand.
- Dirt has a higher potential compactability.
- Dirt has a higher soil strength than sand.
- Dirt *may* be watered less frequently without creating a dust problem.
- Dirt, without proper maintenance, is more conducive to injuries involving bone fractures rather than the soft tissue injuries associated with sand.
- Most dirt arenas will require more frequent working than sand arenas in order to minimize injuries due to hard surfaces.

The natural surfaces found on equine arenas come under the category of soil material whether they are sand or dirt. While the term *dirt* as used for arenas is somewhat misleading, it actually refers in this instance to soil material from varied sources. In all probability, this soil material is mixed with an organic material or materials such as sawdust, bark, peanut hulls, etc., in an attempt to improve the performance of the dirt with regard to water-handling and to reduce the potential for footing problems.

THE NATURE OF SOIL MATERIALS

All of the soil materials that are used for the construction of the arena floor, whether for the surface or the base, were developed on our planet to establish life-support systems for the myriads of plants on the earth, including shrubs, trees, grasses, desert plants, and various crop plants grown under cultivation. These plants grow under a wide variety of environmental conditions, ranging from the arid zone to the humid rainforest. Wherever on the face of the earth these soils occur, certain inherent characteristics allows them to perform optimally, whether supporting the growth of cactus species in the arid zones of Arizona or the growth of mahogany in the rainforests of west Africa.

Soils are not simply an inert mass of weathered rock materials. If we look at the volume composition of a silt loam soil in good condition for the support of plant life, we would find this mass of soil to be made up of fifty percent solids (mineral/organic) and fifty percent pore space. The fifty percent of solid space is made up of about forty-five percent mineral and five percent organic substances by volume. At optimum moisture for plant growth, the fifty percent of pore space is divided roughly in half—twenty-five percent water and twenty-five percent air. Once this same soil has been subjected to traffic—whether it be human, horses, or equipment—the first change is a decrease in the amount of pore space, resulting in soil compaction, which in turn provides a decreased performance of the footing for the equine athlete.

When soil material is used as an arena surface, whether it originated elsewhere or on-site, it becomes subject to repeated compression by the weight of horses and equipment. After the compression is sufficient to produce a compacted surface, maintenance of the arena begins in an effort to get this surface in an acceptable condition for equine performance. How well this surface can be brought back to "life" will depend, in part, on the particular kind of soil material present as well as the method used in working the arena. Soils, with their main role as life support system for plants, possess a number of inherent characteristics—structure, texture, and porosity—to carry out their "assignment." Each dominant soil on the face of the earth has a certain potential or capability to perform with regard to plant growth. The process of using soil as a surface material on an arena destroys its inherent characteristics such as structure and porosity, resulting in a surface that sooner or later requires some help to buoy it up or put more life into it.

The dominant soil materials that are found on our planet are sand, loamy sand, sandy loam, silt loam, silty clay loam, clay loam and clay. Each of these *textures* has a specific range in the percent of sand, silt and clay. (Please refer to Chapters 1 and 2 for more information on soils.)

ADDITIONAL COMMENTS

The term *dirt* when it comes to arenas yields about as much information as kicking the tires does when shopping for a used car. Footing materials for arenas commonly are sand,

Dirt arenas have a higher water-holding capacity than sand. When the arena is worked under wet conditions, the footing can become very deep. Mike Geiger and Chick's Stormy Heart. Photo by Tammy Geiger.

dirt, synthetic materials (e.g., rubber or plastic) or natural, organic products like sawdust, shavings, and peat.

Dirt can differ widely not only from farm to farm but also from arena to arena, particularly when examining indoor arenas. This difference between indoor facilities arises from the fact that usually all the materials for the arena have been brought in. These materials commonly are not uniformly mixed or spread to a standard thickness. Additional materials brought in to finish the arena may appear the same as the original ones, but may vary just enough to cause a significant difference in performance of the equine athlete as well as in maintenance. To address this, other material may be brought in to create a favorable blend with the problem area. Sometimes this works and sometimes it only makes matters worse. You *must* know what you are starting with and the composition of any material you add.

On occasion, the standard analyses available from an agricultural soil testing lab may not answer the question(s) arising in your arena. It may be necessary to go beyond the tests for particle-size distribution (soil texture) and sand-grain size. In one case, a large indoor arena had three different component soils. All three soils tested out as sandy loam with very similar amounts of sand, silt and clay. The problem, however, was in the way each performed with regard to dust, hardness, water-handling, and maintenance. Finally, a test known as the Atterberg Limits was run and pinpointed the problem as being one of difference in physical composition. Although all three soils were indeed sandy loams, one soil had a pronounced tendency for swelling and forming clods when water was added and equipment used. This situation implies a difference in clay mineralogy or clay type. Some clays, Montmorillonite in particular, are subject to swelling when moist and shrinking when dry. The solution to this specific arena's problem was to add washed sand to "dilute" the action of the clay.

5

Turf or Grass Surfaces

TURF CONCEPTS

For outdoor arenas, turf is in a class by itself. It rates high in esthetics, it receives high marks for dust control, and its millions of roots provide the answer for removing surplus water when Mother Nature decides to become overly generous with rainfall.

Why isn't turf used more often? Although grass fields date back to at least the days when lacrosse was played by Indians on foot as well as horseback, those conditions represented native grasses and natural soils. Today, more often than not, we are seeding introduced grass species on man-made soils. These soil materials sometimes overlie subsoil at depths of three to four inches. In some cases, the surface soil has long been removed and the subsoil is at the surface.

A turf arena, at the time of this writing, is only suited for outdoor arenas. The success of any turf for an arena starts at the very beginning, the construction phase, and in particular, with the soil mass, which will serve as the life support system for the grass plants.

SOIL-PLANT RELATIONSHIPS

Grasses, like any other plants, are dependent upon three different soil parameters—chemical, physical, and biological—for their life support.

The chemical parameters pertain to the possible nutrient uptake in solution from the soil. A total of sixteen nutrients are utilized by the plant. The major elements are nitrogen, phosphorous, and potassium; the others, called *trace elements*, are very important but are not needed in large amounts. The essential trace elements are iron, boron, zinc, manganese, copper, molybdenum, and chlorine. For the nutrients to be available to the plants as needed, the soil pH should be in the range of 6.5 to 7.5. In acid soils with a pH of less than 6.5, it may be necessary to add agricultural limestone to bring the pH up to the optimum level.

The physical parameters are soil texture, structure, and porosity. Soil texture refers to the percent sand, silt, and clay comprising the soil matrix. Texture, at least in part, determines how much water a soil will hold, its potential for compacting, the relative ease with which it may be penetrated by grass roots, and the capacity of the soil to hold nutrients for uptake by the grass.

Soil structure refers to the *aggregates* of the soil, whether crumb, blocky, or prismatic, which are held together by the organic fraction of the soil.

The voids between the aggregates units of soil structure are called *pores*. Two size classes of pores are recognized, micropores and macropores. The micropores, visible under magnification, have an important function in providing the soil's moisture in a form available to the plant. The macropores can be seen with the naked eye or under low magnification. The function of the macropores is to enhance drainage of excess water, to carry oxygen for the plant, and to remove by-products of root transpiration, namely carbon dioxide.

The biological parameter is the "life-blood" of the soil and is dependent upon the presence of beneficial microorganisms. This balance of microorganisms plays a significant role in nutrient availability and in enhancing the soil's physical conditions.

SOIL ANALYSIS

Most agricultural soil labs have routine analyses for turf. Depending on the region of the country, these can vary considerably, but basically they consist of tests for nitrogen, phosphorous, potassium, pH, and toxic elements or conditions if common to the area. This type of analysis will guide you in determining the type and amount of fertilizer required. If a state testing lab service is available through the county extension service, this would be adequate. Private labs, if they have a good reputation, could also be used. On occasion, a soil texture analysis could be helpful. This provides the particle-size distribution, or the percentage of sand, silt and clay. If you have a sandy soil (sand, loamy sand or sandy loam) texture, a sieve

Turf facilities can be used for a variety of equestrian events. Turf under light to moderate use is easy to maintain, and has little dust, but freezes and can become too wet. It is also very important to manage correctly; mowing, correct watering management, rest periods, and proper establishment time are all essential requirements for a safe surface. Photo by Dusty Perin.

analysis of the sand fraction could be helpful. This will show the percentage of different-sized sand grains.

SITE ANALYSIS

If you are planning to seed or sod an area for the first time, it is very helpful to perform a soil profile check. This consists of digging a rectangular excavation by hand or with a back-hoe to a depth of eighteen inches or deeper if necessary. The exposed face of this excavation should be as nearly vertical as possible. It is on one of these vertical faces, preferably a south-facing one so natural light is optimum, that a brief soil profile description is made. This entails a narrative description of the different horizons (layers) contained in your soil. One of the more important things to discern is whether your soil is made up of layers with contrasting textures, sandy versus clayey layers, for example. In a situation like this, the soil will likely have an inherent problem with water handling. When two contrasting layers exist next to each other, whether it is a sandy layer over a clayey layer or the reverse, there will be a limitation in the rate water can enter the soil (slow infiltration) and also in the growth rate and ultimate development of plant roots. Such a soil for an arena results in a surface that remains wet after a rain or irrigation and a weak root system giving rise to excessive wear areas, since the sod can be easily ripped out by horse traffic. It is important, therefore, to know what you are starting with. You can then take the steps necessary for soil modification prior to seeding or sodding. You will also know more accurately what management practices will be needed to optimize both the shoot and root growth for improved wear tolerance.

SODDING VERSUS SEEDING

The advantage of sodding compared with seeding is the saving of time for the establishment of a ground cover. While adequate soil prep is needed regardless of whether you sod or seed, another soil factor comes into play when using sod—a suitable match must be made between the soil that came with the sod and the soil where it will be used. The two soil textures, the one on the sod and the other on the field, must be similar enough to be compatible or to assure a good "take." If the sod was grown on a loamy sand and you were planning to install it on a heavy clay loam field, the chances are very high that the sod will not become well established and consequently will have a very short life once equine activity starts. This same loamy sand would have a better match installed on a sand or sandy loam soil and should provide a good take if all its needs are met (irrigation, fertilization, and aerification) during both the establishment and the maintenance phases.

Seeding sometimes has the advantage over sodding based on a more suitable selection of species than may be available from the sod growers. Most often the species and varieties you need for arenas will be the same as those used by the football and soccer facilities in your area. People who manage these facilities may be able to supply you with this type of information. Another source of information could be either the county extension service or the Natural Resources Conservation Service, formerly the U.S.D.A. Soil Conservation Service.

The warmer parts of the United States—those states in the southeast as well as Hawaii—may have suitable grasses that can be propagated from cuttings or sprigs, which are short pieces of stem with one or more nodes that can develop roots and thus spread vegetatively. Those grasses that do not produce viable seed must be propagated by sprigs, if possible.

Regardless of whether you are sodding, seeding or sprigging, providing adequate moisture and nutrient levels is key. Stress, whether due to a lack of moisture or low nutrient levels, can set the stage for weed and insect infestation and disease, further weakening the plant. When the facility is used, weak plants are easily kicked out, leaving bare spots in your surface.

MAINTENANCE

Following the successful establishment of your turf, you become involved in the key area of turf maintenance. Turf maintenance primarily consists of fertilization, irrigation, and aerification. It is one thing to get an effective vegetative cover in the establishment phase, but quite another to perpetuate that plant vigor after equine use has started. The reason for this comes down to basics.

Nutrients

In the establishment phase of turf building, the role of phosphorus is essential. Phosphorus is required for seedling growth and development, and for the development of rhizomes and stolons.

During the period of sodding, a severe phosphorus deficiency can result in the failure of a stand, while ample available phosphorus will enhance by two- to three-fold the coverage of an area by rhizomes and stolons. During the management phase of an established turf, nitrogen becomes more important due to its influence on turf-shoot growth rate and density. When the turf arena is expected to have intense use, increased nitrogen is needed to stimulate turf growth and to fill in divots and thinned areas.

Potassium's role is to increase turfgrass tolerance to environmental stress, reduce the turf's susceptibility to disease and increase its wear-stress tolerance.

Water

Irrigation is both a science and an art. Knowing how much water to apply and when to apply it probably gets more complex as time goes on. The reason for this is two-fold. First, each successive human generation is somewhat more removed than the previous one from a strong relationship with the land. By this I mean that we are increasingly less land dependent, and we are less and less likely to really know how a particular bit of land responds to any given treatment. Second, like any other ongoing field of study, the speciality of irrigation has been invaded by new technology. Irrigation has gone from surface irrigation like furrows and flooding to sprinklers of various designs to electronic timers which schedule water applications through the use of moisture sensors, allowing sprinklers to come on before usable soil moisture is entirely gone and plants go into stress.

There are a number of variables that determine when your grass will need watering. For example,we know that medium- to heavy-textured soils (loams, silt loams, and clays) hold more water than coarse-textured soils like sands and loamy sands. See Table 4.

However, we also know that most often water entry (infiltration) is too fast in sands and too slow in clays for optimum plant growth. Exceptions to this occur. For instance, a water-repellent situation may exist on a sandy soil or a strong structural development with optimum porosity on a clayey soil. With regard to turf, particularly on facilities receiving heavy traffic (e.g., portions of athletic fields, and golf courses, as well as arenas and race tracks), compaction also can be a factor in limiting water intake and should be taken into consideration.

Variables that influence when to irrigate include those factors responsible for higher evaporation and transpiration (that is, sun, wind, high temperatures). The rooting depth of the grass also is a factor. Shallow rooting, for whatever reason, will need to be watered more frequently than more deeply rooted plants. Therefore, it is desirable to encourage deep rooting through species selection and management of the grass.

One of the best methods of determining if irrigation is needed is to take a core sample to a six-inch depth and then employ the *feel test*. (The feel test, developed by the former U.S.D.A. Soil Conservation Service, consists of evaluating the effect of certain moisture levels on the feel, or consistence, of a given soil texture or textures. Please see Chapter 8 for a discussion of the feel test. This method can be readily applied once you know your soil texture. If you aren't sure of the soil texture in the surface six inches of your arena, send a sample to a soil lab and request a particle-size distribution.

Table 4.
Water Holding Capacity.
(inches of water per foot of soil)

Soil	Total Amount of Water Store	Water Available to the Plant
Sand	0.6 - 1.8	0.4 - 1.0
Loam	2.7 - 4.0	1.3 - 2.0
Clay	4.5 - 4.9	1.8 - 1.9

The irrigation of clay soils often requires frequent, shallow applications of water to avoid saturation, which leaves the soils devoid—or nearly so—of oxygen. All roots need oxygen. They use it to make new cells, repair existing cells, and take up nutrients and water. When oxygen is completely cut off, root growth stops, uptake of nutrients, especially of phosphorous and potassium, is almost stopped, and the ability of water to move into the roots is greatly reduced. This is the reason that, after a heavy rainfall on a "tight" soil (one with a slow infiltration), wilted tops can be seen even under standing water. A closer look at the root system often reveals dead and dying roots.

Water—more and more appreciated for the value it represents to all forms of life on our planet—should be used according to the specific needs of the turf. This means knowing your soil, the species, and cultivars, and using preventative maintenance to optimize the conditions for enhancing the turf for your objectives. This maintenance includes fertilization and aerification as required, ensuring that the water that you do apply or the water that comes as rain can be used as effectively as possible.

ADDITIONAL COMMENTS

The use of grass for arena footing is more likely to be successful under one or two conditions. The first (and this is a real "natural" for growing turf) is a natural climate for the growth of grasses. Here I'm referring to a climate similar to those areas in the British Isles where long periods without rain, which can

A Bermuda grass cover on this polo field in central Florida was frequently uprooted during a match. An examination of the root system indicated the shallow rooting depth was caused by a horizontal layer of compaction (marked by the point of the arrow) and poor internal drainage. The roots could not penetrate the compacted layer (the grass normally root at 18 to 24 inches). Divots of grass were uprooted by the polo ponies and were flying all over the field.

cause the plants to go into dormancy, do not occur on a regular basis. A number of the racetracks in Britain are turf because of the favorable climate. While a turf track usually has a lower injury-potential for horses, injury can and does occur on these tracks in cases of compaction and under certain conditions of excess water with its concomitant poor footing. Again, it essentially comes back to a maintenance program—a better term might be "preventative maintenance."

The second condition for the success of a turf arena is a low intensity of use. No guidelines exist for establishing this beforehand. Soil, climate/weather, species of grass used, and management of the facility all play a role in how tolerant a turf facility will be. Recognition of the signs of wear and stress on the grass and then the willingness to grant a rest period until recovery is made are also key for optimum turf cover.

Turf facilities have higher esthetic values and can be more user-friendly than soil facilities, but an understanding of basic agronomy is desirable. If you are uncertain about the agronomy

Left: Bald areas resulting from compacted soil. Right: The same soil in the same field, but this area received crumb rubber and compost prior to seeding.

of your arena, your local extension service should be able to work with you.

Problem Fields

Soil compaction and its adverse effect on the grass cover of a field is not uncommon. While certain soils are more susceptible than others to compaction, the loss of grass cover is the end result. These bald areas will tend to favor ponding of water following rainfall or irrigation.

The soil responses when compaction occurs are:

- A reduction in the amount of water that can enter the soil. In hot weather, this can be critical to plant survival.
- Limited oxygen in the root zone, with die-back of the roots resulting.
- Increased soil strength, making root penetration difficult.
- Increasing difficulty of water utilization by plant.
- Less than optimal soil temperature—either too hot or too cold—for favorable root functioning.

The addition of crumb rubber and compost prior to seeding the grasses can facilitate a more dense root system and a more effective use of water and fertilizer by the plants.

A combination of different equine events may be required from your turf arena; thus, the amount of impact absorbed by the turf is very important. Holsteiners in a combined driving dressage test. Photo by Dusty Perin.

Table 5. Soil Characteristics and Related Problems in Design and Management of Turf Facilities.

SOIL CHARACTERISTICS	IDENTIFICATION	EFFECT ON PLANTS	EFFECT ON MANAGEMENT PRACTICES	TREATMENT*
INHERENT				
Firm in place	Pre-construction	Restricted rooting	Need for drainage and aerification	A, SM
Layering	Pre-construction	Restricted rooting, low vigor	Need for drainage and aerification	SM
Water repellency	Pre-construction	Moisture stress	Need for blending	SM
High water table	Pre-construction	Oxygen stress, chlorosis, stunted growth	Drainage	D
Salt-affected soils	Pre-construction	Stunted growth, low plant density, darker blue-green color, reduced root growth	Drainage and aerification	D, SA

Table 5 Continued

MAN-INDUCED				
Erosion	Pre-construction	Nutrient and moisture stress	Need for scarification	SM
Land leveling	Pre-construction	Nutrient and moisture stress	Extra water and fertilization	SA, SM
Compaction	Pre- and post-construction	Restricted rooting; moisture, nutrient, and oxygen stress	Frequent aerification	A, SM
Water repellency	Pre- and post-construction	Droughtiness	Extra watering	SM
Salt-affected soils	Pre- and post-construction	Stunted growth, low plant density, darker blue-green color, reduced root growth	Drainage and aerification	D, SA

***TREATMENT SYMBOLS:** A = Aerification; D = Drainage; SA = Soil Amendments; SM = Soil Modifications.

NOTE: The treatments listed in the above table are meant only as general guidelines. An on-site analysis is required before a specific treatment can be prescribed.

6

Arena Condition

BACKGROUND

The bands of wild horses in the American West are largely confined to public lands where they eke out an existence shared with other wildlife. This habitat of the wild horse is highly diverse concerning soil characteristics, rainfall, drainage, elevation, slope, aspect, forage, and available water. Managers of these public lands in Colorado and New Mexico strongly emphasize that the wild horses show a definite preference for "softer" lands and tend to stay away from hard, stony land. They also indicate that the prevalence of injuries (whether bone, soft tissue, or hoof) is minimal. Certainly one of the reasons for this is that the horse in the wild can pick and choose his own route since no one is urging him on regardless of the footing.

Good spring grazing in a mountain meadow on the Pryor Mountain National Wild Horse Range in southern Montana. Photo courtesy of U.S.G.S., Biological Resources Division, Chris Papouchis, photographer.

Medicine Hat and his mother amid the rock outcroppings, undulating slopes, and shrubs of Coal Creek, Colorado, in March of 1996. Photo by Marty Felix, Grand Junction, Colorado.

When asked why lameness is rarely observed in wild horses, a researcher on the Pryor Mountain National Wild Horse Range in Montana indicated, "This is possibly a matter of natural selection. Where there are predators in the area, the slow get butchered. It also appears that the sound hoof plays a big role in reducing the incidence of lameness."

The domestic horse confined to an area that is greatly restricted and a footing that can be highly variable is forced to adjust. The degree to which he can adjust depends at least in part on his condition, care, training, and the severity of the footing condition he encounters. We are concerned with this last component.

At least seven factors influence the performance of footing:

- Resilience
- Soil strength
- Depth/thickness
- Moisture percentage
- Texture/particle-size distribution (PSD)
- Gravel content
- Drainage

No attempt has been made to rank these elements in order of importance because the contrasting climates, types and sources of sand, and uses of arenas greatly influence the weight of any factor under consideration.

RESILIENCE

A resilient surface is one that is capable of absorbing a significant portion of the shock rather than transmitting it back to the hoof and leg of the horse. Footing materials that tend to be higher in organic matter, somewhat aggregated, and free of gravel rate high with regard to resiliency. In addition to the footing, the base can also influence resilience or the lack of it. Even good quality sands less than two inches thick over a hard base will tend to show a hard surface due to the lack of cushioning by that thin layer.

SOIL STRENGTH

This term refers to the resistance to movement that soil particles can exhibit when a force is applied to them. An example of two extremes would be a dry sand with low soil strength and a clay with high soil strength.

Soil strength becomes important whenever a horse is executing a turn or he is counting on a firm footing, such as during take-offs and landings in jumping.

Soils of either extreme need to be modified to enhance the skills of the equine athlete as well as to reduce the incidence of injury.

DEPTH/THICKNESS

While uneven thickness of footing is not easily seen without actually gridding the arena, its importance cannot be overstated from the standpoint of performance, safety, and watering. It is not uncommon in an arena designed for a four-inch footing depth for the footing to range in thickness from one and one-half to five inches. Commonly this is due to inadequate or infrequent dragging, particularly with respect to bringing the material back from the rail to the center. The frequency of dragging will depend upon the intensity of use, the texture of the material (fine material travels farther than coarse), and the moisture content (dry materials migrate further). In this respect it should be kept in mind that shallow footing will dry out faster simply because it has less storage capacity for moisture. Thus, the uneven depths of footing also play a role in dust problems.

MOISTURE PERCENTAGE

Sand

The moisture content of soil is responsible for a wide range of conditions. With sandy footings, a low moisture content of two to three percent by weight will control dust for a short period of time but will show little or no difference when compared to dry sand with regard to hardness and soil strength. A medium moisture level of three to five percent will show a longer period of dust control when compared to the low moisture content, and in addition, the sand will tend to be lightly compacted or at least firm. As the moisture percentage increases to five to eight percent, the amount of dust will be controlled for a longer period of time and the surface will become increasingly harder, to the point where many people call this condition "dead"—no spring to it.

Dirt

With dirt facilities, moisture content shows a much wider range of conditions based on the amount of silt, clay and organic matter comprising the footing. Generally the drier end, or low moisture content, of dirt facilities tends to produce a harder surface, while the addition of moisture gives a softer surface. High moisture content on dirt facilities often produces slippery conditions and poor traction. This is especially true when the arena has been allowed to become packed and has not been dragged.

TEXTURE/PARTICLE-SIZE DISTRIBUTION (PSD)

In addition to items described above, a few generalizations can be made. Keep in mind that these are generalizations and that exceptions do occur.

- Soft tissue injuries frequently are more common on sandy footings. Conditions favoring these injuries are

Avoid injuries by critically analyzing your arena footing. Photo from How to Use Leg Wraps, Bandages and Boots *by Sue A. Allen, with permission.*

excessively deep footing and dry to low moisture content.

- Poor traction and fractures are more common on dirt facilities due to the higher soil strength, which does not favor a flexible footing.

Neither of these two injury types is inevitable, but each is more likely when routine maintenance practices are overlooked.

GRAVEL CONTENT

By definition, gravel is any rock or mineral material greater than 2.0 mm in diameter. While some arena people consider gravel a plus in a sand mix, the disadvantages outnumber the supposed advantages. These disadvantages include the potential for stone injuries, particularly if the gravel is angular, increased hardness of the footing and the necessity for more frequent watering to control dust.

DRAINAGE

Drainage refers to the potential of a soil to acquire an optimum level of moisture for a particular purpose. For outdoor arenas, where your facility is subject to nature, high-intensity, short-duration storms or moderate-intensity rains over long periods of time can oversaturate the soil.

Reduction of these wet conditions involves designing your facility to fit its specific environment. Factors such as total precipitation (rain and snow), soil temperature (freezing conditions), storm intensity, and the particular setting of your outdoor facility are important considerations.

- Outdoor arenas need to be crowned with a specific amount of slope or pitch, dependent on your weather data. (See Chapter 10.)
- The base needs to be well compacted to permit water to run off but not erode.
- The sub-base may need to be modified to ensure adequate support.
- The footing should be friable and of uniform thickness to allow water to be absorbed rather than to run off, removing with it part of your footing.
- Low areas which tend to pond water and, subsequently, dry slowly should be avoided.
- Heavy application of organic material should be avoided, since it tends to retain moisture, drying out slowly. Manure with a high straw content is particularly slippery when wet.
- Both low areas and irregular amounts of organic matter will either reduce the recovery time of the arena or set the stage for performance problems.
- Indoor arenas, even though not subject to stormy weather, can also develop drainage problems. These occur through excessive compaction, matted areas of organic matter, breakdown of sand particle size and, on occasion, rupturing of pipelines or malfunctioning of timers on automatic sprinkler systems.

  Localized wet areas, if due to faulty material should be removed and replaced with suitably free-draining material.

  Ruptured pipelines or faulty timers usually will require ventilation of the facility with doors and windows open

Clods are compact, coherent masses of soil usually produced by plowing or dragging an arena that is either too wet or too dry. Depending on the amount of clay in these clods, breaking them down can take a number of equipment passes at the right soil moisture content. The more persistent clods are high in clay and low in organic matter. Camera lens cap shows size comparison.

if temperature and humidity permit. Auxiliary fans and small pumps may be feasible. After the excess free water has been taken care of, it may be desirable to add sawdust to further reduce the moisture level.

ADDITIONAL COMMENTS

If you were to maintain your arena in optimum condition all the time, chances are there would be very little "use" time available. This, of course, is not practical. The other extreme, of course, is to tend to maintenance only when problems of a serious nature arise—troublesome dust conditions or poor performance leading to injury would result, and these are not only unpleasant, but can be hazardous and as costly over time.

Maintaining an arena for performance and safety may not require working and watering the entire arena on a daily basis, but it does require knowing your arena. It's a matter of knowing which areas require extra water, which become slippery with too much water, which contain chronic deep/soft spots and which become excessively hard even with little or moderate use.

When time permits, you will need to make the decision

Standing water on an outdoor arena commonly is due to a low spot over a very tight layer. The water has no place to go until surface drainage is provided. This situation limits the use of the arena and is a potential hazard to the horse and rider.

whether it is best to continue addressing the problem areas as you have in the past or to go ahead and correct these areas through a renovation program.

Three factors commonly related to sub-optimal arena conditions are *time*, *staff*, and *money*. Having enough time to work and water the arena is a common challenge. This is usually a matter of scheduling events too closely. In the case of outdoor arenas, often rain, snow or wind can compete with scheduling maintenance. Sometimes Mother Nature's contribution is helpful, other times it is not, but in either case, she always makes a contribution.

The staff responsible for maintenance needs to be familiar with the facility and have an interest in remedying the situation. It is important to provide more than a Band-Aid approach.

Money is needed to buy the right equipment and to hire the right people to do the right job. In the eyes of a few, money may be the root of all evil, but realistically, money spent in the right way will buy you an awful lot—in this case, an arena worthy of praise!

7

Dust

THE CHALLENGE

The hardness factors of an arena, although easily measured, are difficult to see, and their effects are felt predominantly by the equine athlete. In contrast, dust is a visible problem and it carries a potential health challenge for the equine athlete, the human athlete and the audience in any equine performance facility.

Air-quality specialists classify dust into two broad categories, *respirable* and *settled*. Respirable dust consists of finer particles and is capable of getting beyond the nasal passages and eventually into the lungs. By contrast, settled dust refers to particles of a large enough size that they are trapped in the nasal passages and do not travel into the lungs. In most dust situations, both categories of dust will be present. The percentage of each will depend in part on the age and condition of the footing. Finer particles—very fine sand, silt, clay, and organic matter—are most readily susceptible to becoming airborne. Of additional concern are the amount of silica sand involved and any bacteria, fungi, and toxins that may be attached to the individual particles of airborne dust—a potential for disease.

By definition, dust consists of particle sizes ranging from .001 mm up to .005 mm. Dust may be comprised of either mineral or organic matter, but the greatest part of all ordinary dust is of mineral origin. In addition to footing materials as sources of dust, bedding materials such as straw and shavings and certain feeds such as hay can also make a contribution to the problem. The selection and handling of these materials thus should be kept in mind when trying to reduce dust potential.

In nature, condensing water vapor settles on dust particles and forms water droplets, giving rise to rain or snow. Confined dust, as in indoor arenas, creates some potentially serious problems. The spore stages of certain disease bacteria, for example, can be carried by dust particles. Similarly, mold spores and the pollens which produce hay fever, asthma, and other allergies have as their vehicle airborne dust.

The problem of dust is not a new one to the equine industry. Records indicate that the Greek philosopher Aristotle in 330 B.C. noted a condition of stabled horses called "heaves."[1] Today this common respiratory disease of horses is known as chronic obstructive pulmonary disease (COPD). While equine pulmonary disease is not limited to stabled horses, the likelihood of dust particles serving as the vehicle for this disease focuses the importance of dust abatement in any arena.

ARENA SURFACES

The dust potential for any arena surface material increases with use and age or time. Even the better grades of sand, when subjected to the wear and tear of horses and vehicular traffic for maintenance, are not immune from the abrasion process. At Colorado State University, a physical analysis of the sand immediately following installation and again at eight months following moderate to heavy use showed a significant change in particle size. This lab analysis showed an abrupt drop in the percentages of very coarse and coarse sand particle sizes and a sharp increase in the percent of medium, fine, and very fine particle sizes, as well as an increase in the silt content.

In a sample from the rail area of one of the CSU arenas only two years following installation, the fine and very fine particle sizes in the sand fraction showed a definite increase; a significant increase in the silt- and clay-size particles also occurred. The center area of the arena was sampled separately and showed considerably lower fine and very fine sand sizes as well as less silt when compared with the rail area.

The effects of this increase in the smaller size particles when compared with the sand at the installation appears to be three-fold: First is an apparent settling, somewhat creating a decrease in the thickness or depth of the surface material. Second is an increased dust potential as the silt- and clay-sized particles increase and more readily become airborne. Third, as the material becomes less dominated by the coarser material with its larger pores and becomes increasingly finer with a wider range in particle size—including an increase in silt- and clay-

1. Smith, F.: *History of Veterinary Medicine*, London: Ballieve-Tindall, 1919.

size particles as well as a pronounced increase in fine and very fine sand sizes at the expense of the very coarse and coarse sand—there is a tendency for the sand footing to become more easily compacted.

Keep in mind that any "soil" material, including sand sold for arena footing, will compact. However, the wider the range in grain or particle size, the greater the tendency for compaction. For agricultural soils, the sandy loam textures show the highest tendency for compaction. Consequently, as a sand is subjected to traffic with the resultant abrasive action of sand grain against sand grain, finer particles are formed with the increase in potential for dust and hardness problems.

Dust should be a consideration for horse and rider, but spectators and neighbors, as well, should not be forgotten. Larry Griess and Paint. Photo by Tammy Geiger.

DUST CONTROL

Developing an effective dust control program involves several steps. While a number of materials old and new are on the market, many of these give rise to environmental concerns regarding their use as palliatives. The Arizona Department of Environmental Quality[2] discussed the following materials:

Calcium Chloride

Considered non-toxic but may be toxic to some plants, could become concentrated in groundwater or wells. Care should be taken to avoid contact with eyes or prolonged contact with skin.

Tends to be corrosive to equipment and can create slick areas when surface is wet.

Magnesium Chloride

Same as above but less corrosive than calcium chloride.

Lignosulfanates (a by-product of the wood pulp industry)

Can be moderately toxic to rainbow trout and may cause skin and eye irritations. Creates a slick and a hard surface.

Petroleum-Based Products

May be injurious to skin and eyes.

Surfactants and Enzymes

Generally considered non-toxic; however, they could have a drying effect on the skin, and be severely irritating to the eyes.

USED OIL

Used oil poses a considerable environmental threat because of its heavy metal content and therefore should *not* be used as a dust palliative. Common contaminants of waste oil are potentially very toxic. It has been said that waste oil may

2. *Consumers' Guide to Dust Control Technologies*, June 1989. Prepared for Arizona Department of Environmental Quality, Office of Air Quality, Phoenix, Arizona.

also be carcinogenic, and this becomes increasingly a threat if the oil is taken from waste oil storage facilities where contamination from other materials is a possibility.

DEALING WITH DUST

If you have a dust problem, there is insufficient moisture in the footing. This doesn't mean all the arena is dry, for when as little as ten percent of the surface is dry, dust will be produced. The bigger the area, the more severe the problem.

Insufficient moisture to prevent dust formation can result from several causes:

- Poor water coverage from sprinklers.
- Duration of application insufficient to allow moisture to penetrate the footing.
- High evaporation rate of applied water. Some of this occurs before the water hits the ground in arid climates.
- Hydrophobic conditions of the footing (resistance to wetting). In severe cases, watering for a longer time just creates puddles on the surface.
- Optimum moisture conditions can only come about by checking the moisture level before you start watering and periodically thereafter until you reach a *moist* (but never wet) condition through most of the footing thickness.
- If at all possible, watering should be done in the evening so as to reduce water losses from evaporation due to wind and lower humidity usually found during midday. In addition, water applied in the evening has time to penetrate before the traffic starts. Also, by avoiding high moisture levels at the surface, the tendency for compaction problems are reduced.

CONTRIBUTING FACTORS TO DUST POTENTIAL

The dust potential for equine facilities may be related to any one or a combination of the following:

Type of Material Used for the Footing

Whether the material you are using is mineral (sand or "dirt"), organic (sawdust shavings, peat, or manure), natural, or synthetic, the final answer is based upon a particle-size distribution (PSD) test run in a soils lab. The greater the amount of finer particle sizes in the footing, the higher the potential for dust (see Chapter 13).

Mineral Composition of Sand

Sand can be comprised of a variety of minerals. These different minerals show a considerable range in their ability to withstand abrasion before they break down into smaller-sized particles. Quartz is one of the most common minerals comprising sand and has one of the highest ratings for wear tolerance before breaking down. The feldspars and micas are less durable, breaking down more easily under use in arenas. One of the basic reasons for differences in the sands in various parts of the country, to say nothing about the world, is their different mineral composition. In addition to the variability in wear tolerance, particle shape (rounded versus angular, for example) enters into the picture when it comes to performance of sand as footing material.

Sand Impurities

The amounts of silt, clay, and organic matter in sand are also important factors. An otherwise good grade of sand (mineral composition and suitable particle size) can be further enhanced by the washing process. Washed sand is usually a few dollars more per ton than unwashed sand, but washed sand removes most of the initial dust potential.

Water Repellency

Water handling of the footing can be very important. Sandy materials in particular have long been known to show a resistance to wetting under certain circumstances. Another name for this phenomenon is *water repellency*. The reasons for this are varied, ranging from localized concentrations of organic matter at certain stages of decomposition to abrupt changes in soil texture to compaction to high salt concentrations.

MANAGEMENT PRACTICES

The application of water is the single most frequently used tool for the control of dust. The degree of success that you may have in applying water comes back to two basic considerations:

1) How fast will the water enter the footing?
2) How long will it be retained by the footing?

As mentioned above, some soils have a resistance to wet-

A

B

Dust potential can vary considerably in any arena. Reasons for this include the effective depth of wetting, variability in soil conditions, and the particular event the horse is competing in. Photo B shows relatively low dust created while Photo A has considerably more dust. These two photos are of areas only ten feet apart in the same arena on the same day. A difference in moisture content between the two points is the reason for the dust in Photo A.

ting. When this happens, the person applying the water often assumes the footing material won't hold any more moisture. Actually, the problem usually is one of limited intake. If it were applied slowly enough, the water might filter down three to four inches. The problem with this slow application of water is the total time it takes to water the entire arena.

It must be kept in mind that water cannot move through a soil's solid particles (sand, silt and clay). Rather, water moves around them and through the pores between the soil particles. Pore spaces range in size from very fine to large (micro- to macro-) pores. When the footing has received heavy use, there are fewer pores and they are mostly of the smaller size, limiting water intake.

Other reasons for limited intake may be hydrophobic soils and a high salt content of the water and/or of the soil.

When sprinklers are used, it is usually desirable to have at least thirty percent overlap—fifty percent in some cases—to compensate for the lower application of water which occurs at increasing distance from the sprinkler head.

Sprinkler Considerations

If you plan to use a sprinkler system for watering your arena, the points that need to be addressed include: the size, and shape of the arena, the composition of the surface, climate, water supply, power supply, labor, and management schedules.

Selection of Sprinklers

The rate of water application is determined by the sprinkler head type, nozzle size, nozzle pressure, and spacing of the sprinklers. Each sprinkler head has an optimum range of pressures for a particular nozzle size. When the pressure is lower than optimum, larger drop sizes result and more of the water falls closer to the head. When the pressure is higher than optimum, the water drops are smaller, often resulting in a "mist," with much of the water being lost to evaporation. This is particularly true under arid and semiarid conditions. In some cases volume gun sprinklers have been used in large arenas in order to obtain adequate coverage. This type of sprinkler system is marginal at best. It is definitely poorly adapted to soils with low infiltration rates. For whatever reason(s), low infiltration rates are more often the rule rather than the exception.

For the reasons discussed above, it is not difficult to understand why sprinkler systems are not necessarily a panacea for the watering of your arena. With proper planning, however, very good results can be obtained. Just be sure your installer knows which considerations are key for your arena.

ADDITIONAL COMMENTS

Dust, by definition, consists of dry, solid material particles with a diameter of less than 0.005 mm. One of the indoor arenas at CSU, having an initial sand footing analyzed at 96% sand, no silt and 4% clay, after one year of use was found to contain settled dust with a composition of 26% sand, 47% silt and 27% clay. This illustrates the abrasive effect created by the horses and the maintenance equipment on the footing. The material was airborne before being deposited, making it a candidate for inhalation by horse, rider, and spectator. While water is the most practical means for dust control, there may be considerable value in reviewing your watering practices. Consider the following questions:

- What is your method of water application?
  Sprinklers (moveable, fixed/ground, overhead)
  Water tank on truck
  Hand-held hose
- What changes could you make to benefit your program of dust control? Are wet spots and dry spots common at any given time?
- Regarding these wet spots and dry spots, what will it take to treat them effectively?
- Are you watering at the best time? (Remember, evening is usually best, but whenever it's done, allow ample time for the water to penetrate before using the arena.)

In and around larger or growing cities, outdoor arenas can bring complaints from surrounding home owners. The art of hand watering could become key for dry areas in such cases.

Air quality in your indoor arena is important to all who use it. You can take a shower and shampoo and hose down the horse, but inhaled dust is not so easy to deal with.

One of the benefits of using crumb rubber in a sand footing is that it reduces the abrasion between sand particles (see Chapter 13). However, this only is a benefit when the analysis on the sand shows little abrasion has started. Any footing that is already in a degraded state, with a high content of very fine and fine sand plus a significant amount of silt and clay, will not show any real improvement from adding rubber or any dust palliative.

The following graph shows a comparison of sand grain sizes after a nine month period. The comparision was of sand in an arena that had moderate to intensive horse traffic. As you can see, there is a considerable difference in the composition of the sand. Medium-sized particles of sand increased by 165% while the fine particles of sand increased by 600%. This is a consideration one should take into account when purchasing sand for your new or already existing arena.

A Comparison of Sand Grain Sizes Following Nine Months of Moderate to Intensive Horse Traffic on a Washed Sand Surface.

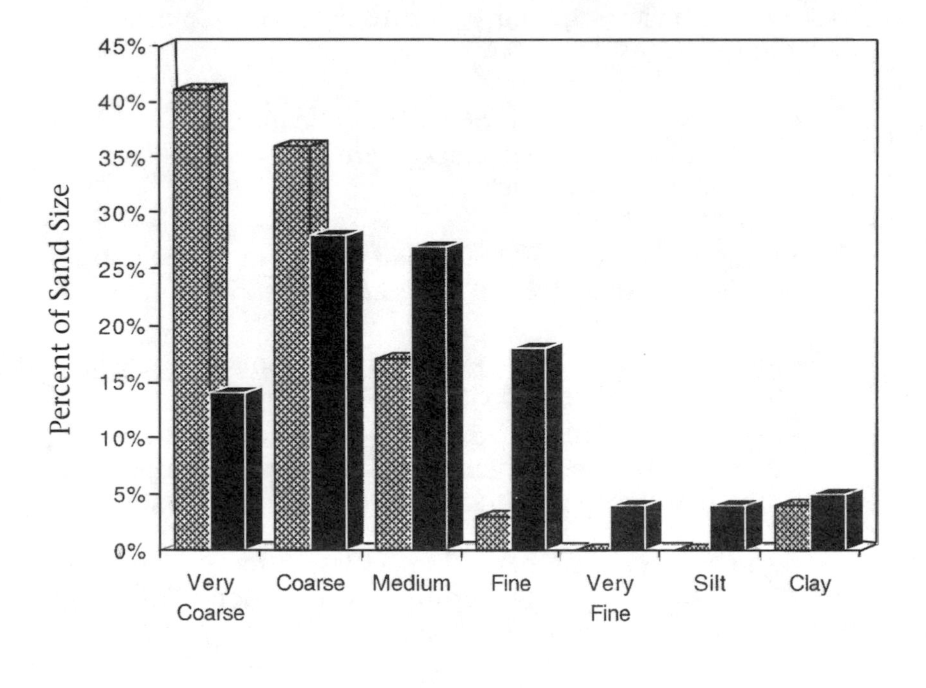

8

Your Water Resource

THE WATER PICTURE

Water is key to optimum arena management. When too little water is applied we set the stage for a dust problem. Too much water, on the other hand, can provide unpredictable footing. When water is applied unevenly, we can have the compound problem of dust in one part of the arena and slick footing in another. In each of these cases, water is being wasted.

The amount of water on the earth at present is the same amount we had thousands of years ago. Today, however, we have many more uses for this same quantity of water. More people, industries, and general overall uses of water can make it a tight commodity, particularly so in periods of drought. We need to become increasingly aware of how we can get along with less in the event the need arises.

The part of the world you live in will determine, at least in part, your concern about water. A considerable area of the Middle East has good supplies of oil, but limited—and highly respected—water supplies. The southwestern United States, much of which is classified as an arid zone, has a climate that attracts retirees in droves, but has limited water supplies. Eastern Canada has an abundance of water and relatively low evaporation rates due to a low incidence of warm, sunny days.

OPTIMUM USE

Equine facilities use water on a regular basis to reduce the dust problem and to improve the performance of their footing, in addition to attending to the biological demands of the animals themselves. Effective watering of a sand or dirt arena consists of watering in such a way as to reduce dry areas, at least in the surface two inches. The most efficient watering can be carried out between sunset and sunrise. This is the time period when losses to evaporation are lowest (with rare exceptions) and thus the water you apply is most effective.

Rather than setting a time limit on how long you will water, you can fine-tune your watering efficacy by first seeing how thick the surface is that requires the addition of water. Use a knife for this and cut several squares with vertical sides to determine the pattern of dryness. Now start your watering and see how long it takes to moisten this dry layer. *Do not exceed this time period*; you will create excessive wetness. Sands that are over-watered will become too firm or "dead."

A suitable guideline for how much water is enough can best be determined using the feel test. Coarse-textured soils (sands, loamy sands, and sandy loams) should form a loose ball under pressure when squeezed in the hand, but not hold together. When more water is added to these soils, a weak ball can be formed that breaks easily. Generally, moisture at this level is not needed; in fact, this moisture level for these soils is conducive to compaction.

Medium-textured soils (loams and silt loams) should be somewhat crumbly and hold together in the hand with pressure. Somewhat higher moisture will form a ball readily and will "slick" slightly with pressure. This last moisture status can be excessive for optimum performance of a turf arena or a standard arena with medium soil textures. It is close to ideal for compaction and may become slippery.

For *turf facilities*, a rule of thumb is that one inch of water per week is required to replace that used by the turf and lost by the soil through evaporation. When natural rainfall fails to deliver this amount, extra increments of water will need to be added by irrigation. One of the more important tools to help determine when to water turf is a soil probe. This tube should be pressed down to a six-inch depth, where it will pull up a core to be examined for moisture content. If the moisture amount is less than optimum, apply the irrigation water to replace the moisture needed. Basic rules include the following:

- Avoid short, frequent periods of watering, which tend to favor shallow rooting of grass.
- Take moisture samples before and after watering to determine if the needed water has indeed been replaced.
- Water between sunset and sunrise to avoid excessive losses to evaporation. In cases where night watering causes the onset of disease, use early morning watering.

- Avoid midday watering. Excessive losses to evaporation and transpiration develop from the sun and wind.
- Avoid watering just before a facility is subjected to traffic (e.g., equine, mowing, fertilizing) to minimize compaction. The exception to this would be when core aerification is planned. At this time, the penetration of the tines are enhanced by a moist soil rather than a dry or wet soil.

For non-turf areas, the basic rules include:

- Avoid over-watering (can produce slick surfaces).
- Avoid under-watering (creates a dust potential, fast).
- If sprinklers are used, it is very important to check moisture penetration.
- The most efficient watering involves additional watering with a hand-held hose with an adjustable spray nozzle to cover dry spots.

The art of hand watering needs to be reviewed because the benefits are undeniable. The most elaborate sprinkler system for an arena cannot be 100 percent effective. Reasons for this may be related to a poorly designed automatic system, textural differences in the footing, and variable thicknesses of the footing.

Assuming you have an arena that is watered entirely by hand, the person doing the watering needs to understand where on the arena the problem areas for water handling are. Some areas require short periods of watering; others seem to have an insatiable appetite for water. With a closer look at these areas, the causes of the problems may become evident, and proper steps then taken to remedy the situation.

Look upon hand watering as being similar to a gentle rain. Remember that water has power. When water is applied at a high intensity, you may finish the job faster, but you may also move the footing, create compaction, and scour the base.

ADDITIONAL COMMENTS

It has been known for some time that the supply of water on our planet is finite. We know what water is made of, but we cannot make it. The number of uses for water increases every year. In addition to industry, there is increased demand for this resource from the growing numbers of people, livestock, pets, and golf courses. Eventually the need to share the water we have will become obvious.

Basically, we need to apply water only in the specific amount required by an equine facility. This is true whether it is a sand, dirt, or turf arena. At the time of this book, automatic sprinkler systems and sensors are not as efficient as the sensing ability of a trained member of *homo sapiens*.

In watering your arena, you are striving for dust control, optimum performance and uniformity. Keep in mind the power of water, and use it appropriately. How closely your watering program approaches optimum will have a strong influence on whether your arena is perceived as a friend or foe.

With increasing demands on water worldwide due to a growing population, the posssibility of water becoming in short supply or more costly is a reasonable forecast. There may come a time when you need more water for dust control in your arena but it may be too costly or not available. Even today in some parts of the arid southwest it doesn't make sense to use treated water for dust control. Is there a resonable alternative? Definitely yes!

The one strategy that keeps presenting itself throughout history is water harvesting. This is a system of capturing rainfall and directing its flow for a particular use. In this case, it would be directing the water into cisterns where it can be used as needed on arenas. This water could also be used for watering trees and shrubs around your facility. One inch of rain on 1,000 square feet of roof yields about 600 gallons of water. In addition to roofs as a catchment, a prepared ground area can also be used.

9

Hardness

THE UNSEEN HAZARD

Studies of ground-related injuries to the human athlete in football, baseball, soccer, and track on natural and artificial surfaces have been under way for at least twenty-five years. Shin-splints on runners and foot and knee injuries in football and soccer are good examples of problems arising from "footing" being in less than optimal condition.

Once the surface material for an arena has been applied and subjected to the usual traffic (horses, tractors, and the equipment for working the arena), the process of compaction begins. The soil material for your surface in the beginning may be composed of fifty percent organic matter and solids (sand, silt, and clay) and fifty percent air and water, in what is called *pore space*. Pores, or voids, are important because they allow air and water movement. Before the traffic begins, this footing has "life" in it, and it feels soft or somewhat resilient. With increased use, any soil aggregates that may have survived excavation, transport, unloading, and spreading become crushed and soil particles become more closely packed together, resulting in reduced pore space. The first pores eliminated are the larger ones. Smaller pores are less efficient, resulting in slower water penetration and, possibly, poor drainage. Just how long this process takes before it becomes noticeable depends on the type and quality of footing you are starting with, the intensity of use, and the moisture content of the footing. The moisture content optimum for compaction is the same content considered optimum if plants were using this moisture, and is commonly referred to as *field capacity*.

THE CONCERN ABOUT HARDNESS

Research at several California racetracks by the University of California, Davis, concluded there is a definite relationship of the racetrack surface to lameness in the Thoroughbred race horse. The placement of a loose top cushion of five centimeters (about two inches) or more can be very effective in absorbing the energy created by the compactive force of the horse. Just how long this cushion stays at an optimum level depends on how well it is worked, the impact of rains, and the uniformity of thickness over the base.

MEASUREMENT OF HARDNESS

An instrument called the Clegg Impact Tester provides an objective measurement of firmness or impact absorption characteristics. This equipment utilizes a drop hammer falling through a tube from a height of twelve inches onto the surface being evaluated. It measures the peak deceleration in gravity units.

In general, good maintenance practices are generally associated with lower impact values. Uniformity of thickness of footing and moisture content are important maintenance concerns. For sand arenas, higher impact values are associated with footing less than two inches thick and also with excessive watering. Soil materials with more silt and clay—commonly referred to as *dirt*—tend to be harder when dry and more resilient when moist.

The Clegg Impact Tester provides a very good means for measuring ground hardness. The black handle is lifted to a given height and the hammer drops to the ground measuring the force of deceleration. This force is recorded as a digital number, which provides a standardized measure of hardness.

CAUSES

Compaction of arena footing materials occurs at a wide range of moisture levels. Nearly everything done in an arena favors compaction. When soils become packed on cropland, athletic fields, and golf courses, the evidence is readily observed through poor plant growth. In arenas, hardness may be observed through poor performance, standing water, and, possibly, injury to the equine athlete.

Most arena surfaces are comprised of sand for various reasons, including its ready availability, reasonable cost, and easy drainage (no "mud"). We need to remember that sands vary in performance based upon their component materials (hard rock, soft rock, coral/shells, e.g.). These materials indicate how much wear and abrasion the sand will handle before it breaks down into finer particles, at which time it can, and often does, perform in a manner considerably different from the sand you started out with.

Keep in mind that any soil will compact or become hard whether it is a sand or a soil with a significant silt or clay content. However, soils with a fairly uniform content of sand, silt and clay have a higher compactive potential than soils made up of particles of about the same size. The probabilities of compaction are given in Table 6 below.

Table 6 makes clear that a number of management practices are critical. Watering should not exceed the limit that the surface will hold (do not saturate), and should be done at a time during the twenty-four hour day that permits the water to penetrate into the surface, with any excess draining downward before traffic (trucks, tractors, tillage, tools, as well as horses) is allowed.

Table 6.
Probability of Compaction.

Low	High
Lower moisture content	Higher moisture content
Soil particles about the same size	Soil particles with a wider range in size
High organic matter	Low organic matter
Light equipment	Heavy equipment

A uniform thickness of the surface material is important to avoid an excessive impact force due to the thinner cushion. This is especially true where a firm base has been designed for the facility.

Excessive hardness is also caused when the base has been inadvertently "grooved" by the use of a disc in working the arena (see Chapter 11). The repetitive use of the disc creates peaks and valleys in micro-relief at the interface between the base and the surface. In addition to the hardness resulting from the ridging of the base material with its higher clay content, discing may create severe unevenness on the base, resulting in footing problems, particularly if the surface is variable in thickness.

Uniform depth or thickness of footing over a firm base is the first requirement for optimum performance. Variable thickness of the footing, a range in soil texture in the footing zone, and a grooved base provide erratic footing, the potential for injury, and less than peak performance.

Four inches of crumb rubber being evaluated in the round pens at CSU. This amount of rubber absorbed seventy to eighty percent of the impact. An additional advantage of crumb rubber in a round pen is its excellent drainage. However, a drainage outlet must be provided for the water to be removed from the base. (See Chapter 10.)

DEALING WITH HARDNESS

Compensating for hardness problems involves several steps:

- Check your surface for uniformity of depth or thickness. A surface shallower than two inches usually implies a high impact potential.
- Check your base by scraping back the surface in problem areas. Does it vary considerably in hardness? Decide whether the soft spots are isolated and can be dealt with by scarification followed by compacting in the moist state. Relatively simple tools such as a hand-held penetrometer can provide you with comparative measurements of the hard versus the optimum base firmness. These penetrometers can be purchased from companies selling soil-testing equipment.
- Finally, check the surface of the base to see if there are grooves created by equipment used in working the arena. Uniformly spaced grooves measuring one-half inch or more in depth should be removed. The best time to do this is when the footing is being replaced. You can also work the arena at right angles to the existing grooves to reduce their height. This will also mix the base material with the footing.

Additional measures to take to avoid developing a hard footing are:

- Work the arena as needed.
- Be sure the footing thickness is nearly uniform.
- Avoid working the arena too deeply, thereby mixing the base material (which has more silt and clay) with your footing.
- Avoid over-watering sand arenas.
- Avoid working or using dirt arenas immediately after watering. This is part of the recipe for making *bricks*, but that is not your objective.

In brief, solutions for hardness range from adding an amendment such as crumb rubber, more effective working of the arena, and using somewhat less water on sands and somewhat more water and/or uniform applications of water on dirt arenas, to removing the footing and replacing it with more suitable material.

ADDITIONAL COMMENTS

Managers of large commercial arenas frequently are required to change the footing periodically, giving the old footing a "rest" before using it again. The rationale for this is to get air into the old footing. Once footing becomes severely compacted, nothing works to fluff it up again like breaking it up and putting it to rest. This process breaks up the compressed materials, allowing air to permeate. When placed down again, the footing once more stands "higher" than it did after compaction had set in. This general process also rids old footing materials of excess ammonia concentrations.

The heading horse is absorbing all of the shock through his left front leg (arrow). The footing should be designed to minimize this type of impact to the equine athlete. Mike Geiger and Tiny, photo by Tammy Geiger.

10

Outdoor vs. Indoor Arenas

Obviously, the outdoor arena is much more dependent on Mother Nature than the indoor arena. For this reason alone, outdoor arenas provide shorter periods of optimum use, particularly in areas where wind, heat, cold, snow, or rainy seasons can be expected.

SITE SELECTION

The rating of factors of importance for locating an outdoor arena is difficult because of large differences in soils and climate. Certainly topographic position, soil, and climate are the basic factors to be concerned with.

Topographic Position

Your site must be high enough not to be inundated by flood waters. These could arise from seasonal run-off from adjacent slopes, peak flows of streams, inundation from flood irrigation or too close a proximity to wetlands, at least seasonally.

Soil Characteristics

Depending on whether you are planning a low-cost, basic arena on an existing surface or a maximum performance arena with a sub-base, base and footing construction on the surface, soil characteristics vary in importance. The first characteristic to be considered is *soil texture*. This term can be described as the percentage of sand, silt, and clay in a given soil sample (see Chapter 3). Textures are grouped into the following:

- Coarse textured—sands and loamy sands.
- Light textured—sandy loam.

- Medium textured—very fine sandy loam, loam, silt loam, and silt (these textures contain moderate amounts of sand, silt, and clay).
- Heavy textured—sandy clay loam, clay loam, silty clay loam, sandy clay, and clay (a noticeable increase in silt and clay content with somewhat lower sand contents).

Generally, the heavy-textured soils provide a suitable base and sub-base. The coarse-textured soils are preferred as the footing.

An additional concern is the soil's ability to handle water. This becomes a factor especially when building a low-cost facility where there is a need for the ground to absorb the rain that

Indoor arenas are managed very differently from outdoor ones. Photo courtesy of James Arrigon.

comes down. Ground that is not naturally well-drained will have considerable periods of non-use due to either high rainfall or heavy snow melt.

If you are constructing a moderate- to high-spec arena, the base and sub-base will need to be packed and thereafter they need to "shed" the water falling on them. To accomplish this requires either a crowned or a sloped surface which will provide for a controlled run-off so as to remove excess water and permit use as soon as possible after watering. The maximum slope of one to two percent will remove the water without removing the footing, barring a downpour of long duration.

So-called "cracking clays" are soils that shrink when they are dry, causing cracks to develop of up to one to two inches wide and several feet deep. These cracks can be hazardous to the horse, and the soils must be properly managed to minimize their occurrence. Applying water will cause these soils to expand, thereby closing the cracks. Working in large amounts of organic debris, and possibly crumb rubber, may help stabilize the soil. The application of these materials may become a routine practice as needed.

Climate

Arena facilities can be found anywhere man has settled. Consequently, facilities exist in a wide variety of climatic conditions, from the cold subarctic to the hot and humid tropics to the hot and dry arid zones. These three broad zones represent a wide range in precipitation (rain and/or snow), temperatures, day length, periods of use versus non-use, and soils. The management details required for each of these conditions also vary greatly. In some of these areas, the soils may be dry for only two or three months per year. In certain tropical areas, soils may be present that are inherently slick due to a certain clay mineralogy. In arid areas, the need for water to keep the dust under control may be a major concern. In the subarctic, frozen ground limits the period of optimum use. In this same area, frost heaving may also be a problem, making stone removal a routine chore. Research in the mountainous areas of Idaho indicates that soils with a high silt content are more subject to frost heaving. The attempt here is not to describe in detail what will be found in these different areas, but to highlight some of the significant points.

All of the considerations described above will have a bearing on the two management practices of dragging and watering. The arid and semiarid zones have a higher water demand than the humid tropics, for example. In arid and semiarid areas where water is either scarce or too expensive to use as needed, innovative means of water management may be required. These measures are currently being evaluated for their application on arena facilities. At the time of this writing, these methods have not been sufficiently tested. High rainfall areas have fewer windows for working the arenas at an optimum moisture content. For outdoor arenas in these areas, drainage will be key.

While the site selection for an indoor arena involves some of the same concerns, namely topographic position and soil characteristics (for a firm base), the sites differ primarily in that one is protected from the elements and the other is not. In temperate climates, the indoor arena is shielded from climatic extremes (snow, rain, and wind) and their effect on the footing, the base, and management practices. However, dust levels for indoor arenas can reach the hazardous level because of the enclosed structure. (See Chapter 7.)

MANAGING THE ELEMENTS: SUN, WIND, SNOW

While there is essentially nothing we can do to change the climate, there is a very meaningful way that we can modify the elements. Outdoor arenas receive the full impact of the sun, wind, snow, and rain whenever these elements are present. Man has the tools to alter the effects of sun, wind, and snow through the use of windbreaks. (Rain will just have to be taken as it comes.) Windbreaks can provide snow control to improve working and recreational environments, as well as providing visual screening and dust control.

> Farm and ranch windbreaks provide the greatest benefits in areas with high winds and large amounts of snow, extreme temperature fluctuations or minimal natural forest cover. Traditionally, the most extensive use of ranch and farmstead windbreaks in the United States is in the Western, North Central and Great Plains regions.[1]

Windbreaks have been used for many years for the protection of farmsteads, fields with soils subject to wind erosion, and more recently, the protection of feedlots. Their use on areas adjacent to outdoor arenas, however, is not a common practice, but the need is very real. The benefits of a designed shelterbelt next to an outdoor arena where high winds, snow and extreme temperatures occur include increased comfort for the rider as well as the equine athlete, increased effectiveness of water applied to the arena, reduction of snow accumulation, lowered potential for "nuisance" dust in or near residential neighborhoods, and, finally, increased esthetics of the facility.

Planting a windbreak should start with the assistance of the local forest service. This office can provide you with an effective design for your specific site, information on preferred species to use and where to obtain them, and planting instructions, including the best time of year to plant.

ROUND PENS

Footing in round pens seldom gets the attention it deserves. The term *deserves* needs to be emphasized because

---

1. *Windbreak for Rural Living*, by Brace Wight, Soil Conservation Services, James R. Brandle, University of Nebraska.

Snow can and does cut your usable time for your outdoor arenas. Snow management by the use of a designed windbreak can greatly reduce the problem of drifting snow and the residual moisture when it melts.

this is where the young horse should be allowed to concentrate on learning rather than dealing with incompetent footing.

The same considerations that have been identified for arenas in general also pertain to round pens. The differences arise from the concentrated traffic in round pens and the generous amount of side-cast material which requires pulling back toward the path on an as-needed basis.

In addition, most round pens, being outdoor facilities, are subject to the whims of Mother Nature. Standing water, dust, excessive hardness by compaction, or, in some cases, freezing or frost action all put an extra strain on the suitability of the facility. In warm climates (both arid and humid zones), shade either through the benefit of a tree canopy or a location on the north side of a building can improve the temperature within the pen for the trainer as well as the horse. This partial shade will also reduce the moisture evaporation from the footing which will, in turn, reduce the dust potential.

The need to provide adequate drainage is very important in order to optimize a user-friendly footing. In temperate climates, whenever excess moisture is trapped within the footing

Standing water in round pens can reduce the usable size of this facility and increase the hazard of injuries. Drainage can prevent the problem and is not costly to install.

and the temperature is above freezing, an unstable footing results. When this same excess moisture is trapped in the footing and temperatures fall below the freezing mark, excessively hard footing is the result, with potential injury to the equine athlete. Hardness measurements of over 600 have been observed on frozen footing in round pens. (The Japan Racing Association considers a level 125 to be acceptable, according to a report entitled "The Science of Safety," by Les Sellnow, *Blood-Horse,* Sept 7, 1991). To make this situation worse, only part of the pen, commonly about fifty percent, will be frozen and very hard while the remaining portion will be in various stages of "softness." Round pens constructed with solid panels very definitely favor snow accumulation due to the shadow created by the panels. This snow commonly occupies one-half of the area within the round pen. This same area favors frost or ice formation.

A definite requirement for any round pen is the provision of drainage through the use of perforated pipe. Extreme care must be exercised in positioning the pipe to avoid endangering the horse or exposing the pipe to the use of equipment. A very porous, well-drained footing material, such as sand plus rubber, also could provide the drainage needed.

Round pen construction using heavy, solid panels tends to act as a dam, catching all the water running into it. The result is either ponded water, with concomitant deterioration of the base and the footing, or, in colder weather, a sheet of ice. To reduce the likelihood of these events, a Hickenbottom Intake with a Bar Guard on the top of the intake/riser is recommended.

The use of a four-inch crumb rubber footing in outdoor round pens is being evaluated at the time of the printing of this book. A number of factors led to use of straight crumb rubber for this purpose. Among the arguments for the use of rubber include a reduced impact to the equine athlete, little, if any, watering required for dust control, easier maintenance, and a longer season of use (see Chapter 13).

Reduced impact was clearly demonstrated, with Clegg readings in the range of 20-40. When sand or dirt was used in these same round pens, Clegg readings of 200-300 were commonly observed.

Dust in a round pen can be overwhelming when the right materials exist. This is because the relatively small area of footing tends to receive more than its normal share of pounding hoofs, and the associated abrasive action creates a high dust potential.

Primarily, maintenance involves pulling the side-cast material back onto the zone of traffic. Crumb rubber is a very light material, and consequently the amount of effort required to pull it away from the panels is relatively low.

Straight crumb rubber can extend the season of use of a round pen. However, drainage must be built into the lower end of the pen; otherwise, water will accumulate and tend to penetrate the base. This creates a mixture of the base material with the crumb rubber in the saturated zone, which results in a smaller area available for use or a lower efficiency of this footing when it is not submerged, or nearly so, in water.

Meeting the requirements for a straight rubber round pen involves an adequately constructed base that is generally impermeable to water, and a one to one and one-half percent slope with a drainpipe against the panel to dispose of the accumulated water. The size of the crumb rubber ideally would be one-half inch minus, with a range of one-quarter to one-half inch in diameter. Some one-eighth-inch materials can be included. This material must be metal-free. Make your purchases from a reputable dealer.

The first introduction to crumb rubber at the colt training class at CSU.

The amount of rubber needed is calculated by multiplying the number of square feet in your pen by the weight of the rubber per square foot. Crumb rubber ranges from 30 to 32 lbs. per cubic foot. At the CSU round pens with four inches of footing, this came to about 10.0 lbs. of crumb rubber required per square foot.

Getting used to a straight rubber facility can be a new experience for horses. Rather than the usual "jolt," they feel a pronounced springiness. While it is not yet known whether four inches is the best depth of footing, it *is known* that two inches of crumb rubber will not provide the cushion desired, and that depths greater than four inches may subject the horse to soft tissue injuries.

ADDITIONAL COMMENTS

In general, the required management practices are less for indoor arenas than for outdoor ones. The bottom line is that indoor arenas allow better protection from the elements. Sun, wind, temperature, rain, snow, hail, and humidity all have direct access to the outdoor facility. Sun, wind, and low humidity all contribute to an increased rate of moisture loss. Conversely, rain, snow, and hail can create excess moisture, resulting in poor performance and pointing to the need for improved drainage. Site selection is key for outdoor arenas. Avoid topographical depressions where water can collect and take its toll on the base of the arena as well as the footing.

In indoor arenas, the benefit of being able to control the moisture of your footing is a distinct advantage when attempting to obtain optimum performance. Keep in mind that sand footing becomes softer as it becomes drier. The so-called "dirt" arena tends to become softer in the moist state.

Arena conditions can change from day to day. The arena floor should be checked before every equine performance event, to adjust for the day-to-day variations. Photo by Dusty Perin.

11

Arena Maintenance

— With Kevin Hodges

THE VALUE OF MAINTENANCE

Arena maintenance, for most of us, usually is performed as the need arises. Indicators such as holes, wet spots, hard areas, dust, and slick areas get our attention; then we select the appropriate remedy and fix the problem. Unfortunately, by the time the problem is apparent to us, some of its influence may already have been felt by the equine athlete. The effect of this influence may be subtle, as in a soft tissue injury, which may result in the animal holding back instead of feeling confident and going for the gold.

The purpose of working the arena is threefold. First, it is important to modify the surface several inches to favor the circulation of air. By doing this, we create something of a cushion, reducing any excessive concussive force. Second, we aim to leave the soil in a condition which favors moisture intake and its retention for an appreciable time to reduce the dust potential. Third, working the arena should tend to increase the uniformity of the footing, reducing differences in depth or thickness, hardness, and slick spots and developing an overall consistency.

Some of the more subtle problems with arena footings involve a variable thickness, with the resulting hardness of the shallower footing being transmitted to the leg of the equine athlete. Differences in thickness of the footing, moisture content, and composition (percent sand, silt, clay and organic matter) can alter the soil strength, increasing or decreasing the reliability of the footing for the equine athlete. These are termed "subtle" problems because, for the most part, they develop slowly and almost imperceptibly over time. In some cases, it is the horse that identifies the problem before the rider is aware of it.

SOIL COMPOSITION

Soil has four basic components, and the percentage of each will vary considerably depending on whether we have a sand or dirt arena. Assuming we have a dirt arena, as represented by a typical sandy loam soil for example, the volume composition would be represented by the percentages as shown below.

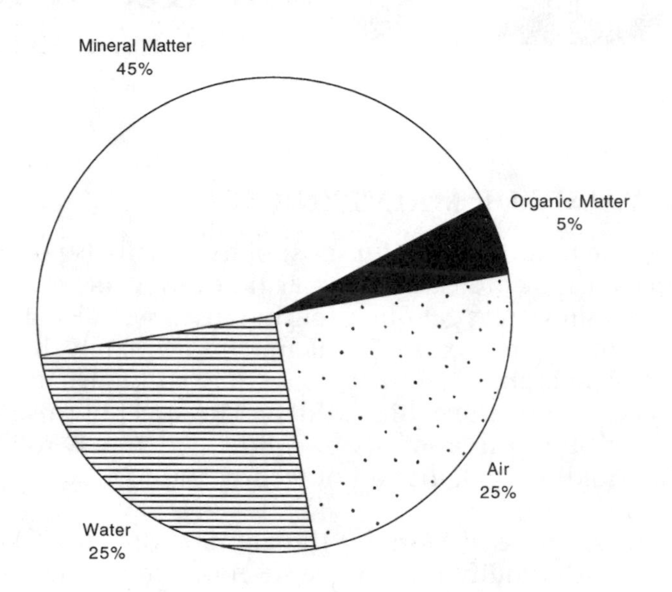

Four components (volume composition) of a typical sandy loam soil. Following horse activity on this "ideal" soil, particularly if it is somewhat moist, soil compaction occurs, reducing the pore size and the amount of air in this soil. The result is an increase in the weight of the soil. We then have a footing which handles water poorly—producing a surface that is either too wet or too dry. If it is too wet, a slippery footing results; if too dry, there is an increase in the time and effort necessary to get the footing back into a suitable condition. Most importantly, this hard surface has a potential for injury to the horse.

From the physical point of view, the mineral component is comprised of three fractions: sand, silt and clay. The sand particles are visible to the naked eye and provide a "gritty" feel to the soil. Sand has a very low water-holding capacity and a very low soil *strength,* the ability to resist a force pushing against it. Silt particles can barely be seen by the naked eye. They have a smooth feel to them, similar to that of flour. Soils with the largest "available" water-holding capacity are characterized as being high in silt. On the negative side, silt has a high dust potential when dry. The clay component has the smallest of the three particles (see Chapter 3, Table 1). Most clays feel sticky and plastic when wet and hard when dry. Their water-holding capacity is high, but not all of this moisture is available to plants, a factor important when estimating irrigation requirements for grass arenas. Soils high in silt and clay are more subject to compaction with resulting hardness. In addition, high silt and clay soils often require primary tillage rather than just dragging, as in the case of sand arenas.

SOIL TEXTURE

Texture is the relative proportion of the various size groups of individual soil grains (separates). See Table 1 in Chapter 3, where the names of the separates are given, together with their diameters and the number of particles in one gram.

TOOLS OF THE TRADE

The type of grooming equipment that you select depends in part on affordability and what your specific needs are, that is, what type of soil is in your arena and its current condition. The following types of equipment represent a wide range in price as well as capability.

The spring-tooth harrow has limited value by itself as a grooming tool. It was originally designed for use on rocky, rough ground. When used on compacted areas, the spring-tooth frequently leaves a cloddy surface that still has to be dealt with.

The spring-tooth and spike-tooth harrows are both considered drag-type harrows. These implements are useful for secondary tillage and are primarily used for "grooming." This is in contrast to the disc harrow, which is more expensive, more complicated, and is useful in breaking up firm soils. The spike tooth harrow requires one-third to one-fifth of the draft requirement of the spring-tooth harrow. The spring-tooth does have an advantage in rough or stony ground and will penetrate up to seven inches, which helps to loosen clods and stones and bring them to the surface. These conditions are seldom relevant for arenas.

THE USE OF THE DRAG

The reasons for dragging will vary to some extent by the type of footing present. Briefly, dragging should be done on an as-needed basis to redistribute the footing. The usual problem is that rail areas become too shallow due to rutting and side-cast material, while the center tends to build up in thickness. The change in depth for sand footing will vary with the nature of the sand and the dominant events held in the arena. This requires redistributing and leveling the footing as needed, using

Some of the earliest tools used for arena grooming were aimed primarily at smoothing the surface—basically a cosmetic effect. This type of equipment is still in use today. One version is made from angle iron welded together, with bolts or railroad spikes mounted in the framework. Additional weights are often used to increase penetration. Even with the extra weight it is difficult—if not impossible—to maintain a uniform depth of penetration. There is a tendency for this equipment to skim over the top rather than to dig effectively into a hard surface.

a tractor and a drag. In addition, footing that has migrated outside the arena fence will need to be pulled back in. Failure to do so will subject the material in the rut along the rail to excessive abrasion, creating a high dust potential, a higher probability of compaction after watering thus creating a poor footing and exposing the horse to potential injury, and poorer drainage.

SELECTING THE RIGHT HARROW

Harrows, whether spike-tooth or spring-tooth, can be very effective tools. The preference of one over the other depends on whether your arena is sand or dirt. In dirt arenas, the spike-tooth may be preferable if the soil is in a cloddy condition and these clods need to be broken up.

In the case of sandy arenas, a chain drag or a home-built chain-link drag may better fit your needs. Basically, the type of equipment used is determined by whether you need to level high points or you need to break some clods.

If you have a shredded wood or bark surface, a chain-link harrow without spikes will work well to level, rather than dig into, the footing. These types of materials are meant to remain on the surface rather than be worked into the footing.

The types of equipment used to groom arenas are quite diverse and are beyond the scope of this book. Facilities vary by region of the United States and equipment often is tailored to fit a specific need.

The disk harrow is most commonly used on outdoor "dirt" arenas that are subject to becoming very compacted. This harrow has the disadvantage as a grooming tool in that it creates a compacted zone at its depth of penetration. It also frequently provides a grooved surface on the base.

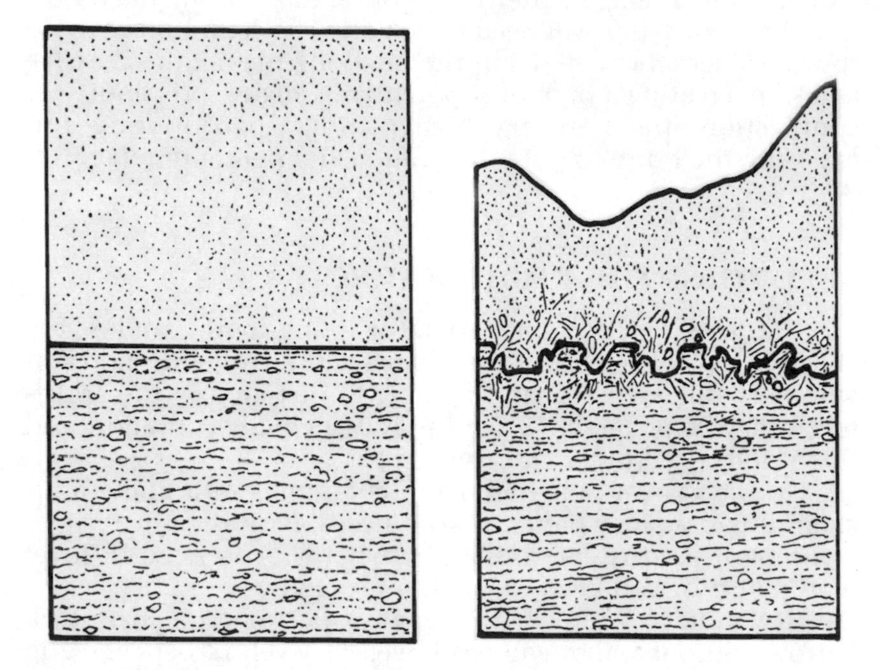

On the left is an undisturbed cross-section of an arena floor showing uniform depth of footing overlying a smooth base. The drawing on the right shows what commonly occurs when equipment is used to work the arena while assuming the footing/surface is of a uniform thickness. In the shallow areas of the footing, the equipment digs into the base, causing an uneven base and causing the base material to be mixed with the footing material. This situation not only contributes to the dust problem, due to the higher silt and clay content coming from the base, but it also increases the potential for injuries due to lack of a uniform surface on the base.

A number of points need to be emphasized concerning the use of any equipment in working the arena:

- **Compaction**—Tractor wheels do exert a compactive force on the footing. This force will vary in intensity depending on the moisture content, the texture, and the condition of the footing. The compaction can be compensated for while dragging by being sure the drag extends beyond the width of the tractor wheels. Practices such as watering with a water tank pulled by a tractor do leave compacted areas.
- **Protecting your base**—Periodically, it is desirable to remove your footing in several small areas to determine if the dragging has dug too deeply. Very often when this

happens, grooves will be observed in the base, resulting in the mixing of silt and clay from the base into the lighter-textured footing. In extreme cases, grooves develop of such dimension so as to provide unstable footing for the animal, creating a possibility of injury. This situation is quite common on dirt arenas where a disc harrow has been used. Where sand footing exists over a clay base, correcting this may require removing the footing, working up the grooves, compacting the base and replacing the footing.

To avoid the grooves in the first place, it is necessary to know the thickness of your footing, be sure your drag does not extend deeper than that footing, and finally, avoid working the arena in the same pattern. Then, on the occasion that you do exceed your depth, the chances of grooves developing in the base are minimal.

- **Tools**—The use of a three-point hitch as opposed to a free drag attachment requires a higher level of expertise in the operator. The three-point equipment is generally more aggressive in the soil compared with a drag such as a mulcher, harrow or chain rake. The three-point implement follows the relief of the ground inversely to the

This type of grooming tool operates from a three-point hitch on a tractor. It rotates in a circle, causing the teeth to break up the surface. The operator can adjust the depth of penetration as well as angle of the equipment to level out areas of deeper footing.

The Arena Groomer, from Parma, attached to a tractor with a three-point hitch, can be adjusted for variable depths of penetration. It has tines for loosening compacted areas, a leveling bar for moving the footing around for a more uniform thickness, and a roller bar in the rear to break up clods. By being able to regulate the depth of penetration, there is less chance of digging into the base and creating performance problems. Photo courtesy of Parma Co.

front of the tractor. Thus, when the front of the tractor goes up, the implement digs deeper, and conversely, when the front of the tractor goes down, the implement may come out of the ground. A three-point attachment generally requires a heavier, more powerful tractor, but can accomplish the job faster because it can be forced into the ground. A drag attachment can do a satisfactory job, but it is limited by its own weight as well as the hardness of the soil. For this reason, the drag can take longer, particularly on dirt footings because it requires more passes to develop a uniform, or consistent, surface.

GENERAL

Suitable footing materials should break and fluff up quite readily. In outdoor dirt arenas, it is not uncommon for large clods to be evident when equipment first is used on them. This usually is a result of "foreign" soil material being added to the original inadvertently or because it "looked okay."

To achieve the ideal physical state in an arena requires first of all that you have a soil material that lends itself to being worked. At the top of the list is a soil low in silt and clay and high in sand, with at least a four to five percent organic matter content. Moisture content should be low so that smearing or balling up does not occur. Keep in mind that *any* soil will compact when subjected to traffic. A sandy loam texture is one of the more easily compacted soils, but when subjected to traffic—whether equine or equipment—at a *low* moisture content, compaction will not be serious.

When dragging an arena, the fewer passes necessary to get the job done, the better. Reduced wheel compaction potential and increased efficiency of the operation (in time and fuel consumption) are two strong points in favor of this approach.

In working sand arenas, particularly those on compacted bases as well as those on prepared bases, the uniformity of the footing thickness is very important. With either type of base, a footing of two inches or less increases the potential hardness factor, creating a hazard for the equine athlete. An inexperienced equipment operator (or one assuming the arena has a consistent thickness of footing), will leave his imprint in the base either in grooves or in mixing some of the base material with the footing. Silt, in particular, is a heavy contributor to dust problems, along with very fine sand, and should not be stirred up from the base.

Side-cast material from heavy use of the rail area will need to be pulled back to avoid further deterioration of the base. This is really a preventative maintenance procedure. A rail area that is neglected or where corrective action is delayed invites injuries from its existing hard surface. This may also be a poorly drained area, where water collects due to the compacted surface caused by degradation of the sand, which now possesses increased fine and very fine sand grain sizes mixed with some silt and clay from the base.

SPECIAL CONSIDERATIONS FOR OUTDOOR ARENAS

Outdoor arenas are more vulnerable than indoor facilities to weather (meteorological events on any given day) as well as climate (meteorological events throughout the year). Some of these challenges include the following.

Rainfall

High-intensity, short-term, as well as low-intensity, long-term, storms can create problems for outdoor arenas. To minimize damage from these types of rain, we need to look at both on-site and off-site damage potential. On-site damage occurs when the amount of rain falling is greater than the storage capacity of the footing. Most sandy footings are low in storage capacity, and when this capacity is exceeded, run-off or ponding occurs. Run-off results when the slope of the arena exceeds the rule for your geographical area. Ponding results when water collects into areas of depression and remains there until absorbed, channeled off, pumped off, or Mother Nature helps with a drop in humidity and increased winds. In some cases, run-off from the surrounding areas may be the cause of most of the water on the arena itself. To avoid this, diversion ditches may be situated above your arena to avoid run-off from the slopes above. Slopes contributing run-off to your arena need not be precipitous—a slope of three to four percent can deliver a lot of water during a moderate rain. The Natural Resources Conservation Service may well be able to assist you in assessing the need for and design of the diversions.

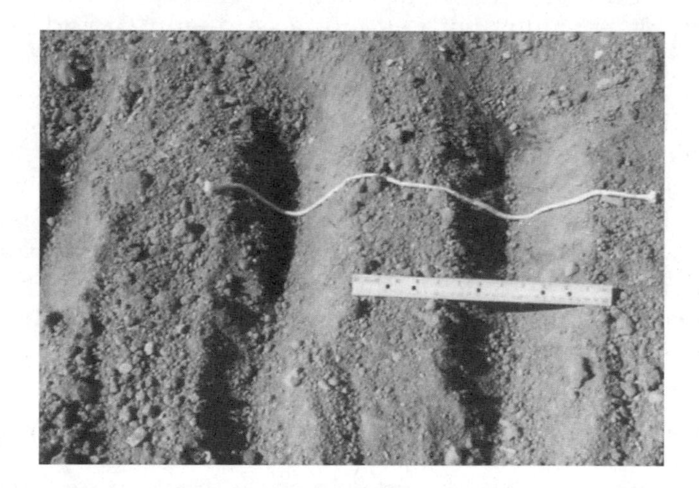

The surface material was pulled back to reveal the "ridge-and-valley" phenomenon in the base. This configuration was caused by ripper teeth on a drag. This arena, like so many outdoor arenas with a surface soil of sandy loam, compacts easily. For this reason, some ripper action was necessary, but here the depth of ripping was excessive. The width of the "valley" varied from 2 to 4 inches; the depth from 3 to 4 inches. Unstable footing results—and unstable footing is probably the least serious consequence you can expect from this situation.

Low Temperature

Whenever the cold temperatures of winter have begun, the potential for frost action beneath the arena arises. Frost action, particularly the freezing and thawing beneath the surface, can create frost heaving which can bring rocks (gravel and cobbles specifically) with diameters of up to eight to ten inches to the surface. This phenomenon is common in the northern half of the United States. Frost heaving becomes increasingly common with increased elevation. According to research carried out in Idaho, an even greater tendency for this exists in mountains where the soil texture has a pronounced silt content.

Wind

Wind can either warm or chill a horse and rider. Equally important is its effect on the arena. In the west, chinook winds during the winter and spring can reduce a snow pack on an arena almost before your eyes. Similarly, a hot, dry wind can create a dusty arena as it picks up moisture and transports it elsewhere.

To reduce the potency of wind action, windbreak plantings may be of use. In many areas, planting stock is available at a nominal fee from state nurseries. Help in the design of the windbreak may also be available from the local extension service or the State Forestry office.

ADDITIONAL COMMENTS

The old saying "The eye of the master fattens the flock" applies to arena management. When you observe something in the footing that isn't performing to your standards, deal with it, don't ignore it.

Water plays a key role with regard to obtaining optimum footing conditions. Too much can create a surface that's either too hard or too slick. Too little moisture can be the cause of excessively deep footing, poor soil strength, and finally, dust.

An optimum organic matter content can improve the condition and performance of most footings. Finding the right level of organic matter for the condition and type of footing you have is important. It is best to start by adding a small amount and increasing that amount slowly until you get something that works for you. A very high organic matter level can weaken the soil strength and create slick conditions when wet. If you inadvertently add too much organic matter at once, it will oxidize in not too long a time, when it will again be necessary to add more.

The decision to change your footing or to modify it by adding sand or some other amendment should only be done when your maintenance is all that it can be! Remember, no chain is stronger than its weakest link.

The combination of proper working of the arena, water application, and composition of arena materials will result in a well conditioned surface that is optimal for various performance events. Tammy Geiger and Mr. Scat Bar. Photo by Sherry Geiger.

12
The Holistic Approach to Arena Management

KNOW YOUR STARTING MATERIALS

The two most common problems in arena management are dust control and dealing with hard surfaces. Ideas for solving these problems include more frequent watering and regular working of the arena. In addition, a growing number of new products have reached the marketplace, many with quite convincing-sounding claims for solving your problems.

Most of the materials used for footing in arenas are natural, sand being the most common and extensively used. So-called "dirt" is also used, but sand is considered easier to manage. Whether sand or dirt, certain problems arise for any facility. These problems need more than a Band-Aid approach, and the only way to achieve this is through understanding what you are dealing with. This does not put arena management in a unique position, but, rather, in one similar to any technology where alternatives to a conventional management are considered.

Holistic management was proposed in the 1980s as a way to manage ecosystems under stress from human activities. Basically, this approach emphasizes the interconnectedness of all things. For example, sands vary in the way they handle water. For this reason, some sands require daily watering while others may go several days between watering before dust becomes a problem. Some sands compact very hard; some never reach this hard state. These differences can occur in any given arena, largely due to zones of varying intensities of use.

The interactions in natural footings are complex. We see the "effect," but the "cause" is usually confirmed by certain laboratory analyses or, in some cases, on-site testing. The most common lab analyses are the particle-size distribution (PSD) and the sand sieve or sand separate analysis. The PSD provides you with the percentage of sand, silt, and clay. The sand sieve analysis shows the percentage of each of the five sand sizes (very coarse, coarse, medium, fine and very fine) making up the sand portion of your footing.

What bearing does this have on how well your footing performs and responds to management? Relatively small quantities of silt and clay can accumulate at points of sand particle contact and begin to seal off the pore channels necessary for water movement. This is one of the reasons why a sandy footing may have drainage problems. In sands, the maximum silt content should be limited to less than five percent and the clay content to less than three percent by weight.

Very fine sands (0.10 to 0.05 mm particle diameter) retain more water than do coarser sands and may provide poor drainage, particularly in outdoor arenas.

Hydrophobic sands, those showing a water repellency or

Don't forget to address problem areas in your arena. These may include: ruts on the rail, ruts from longeing horses, barrel racing ruts, dry spots, and wet spots. Photo by Dusty Perin.

resistance to wetting, can be a problem. This situation is more common on older arenas where organic matter has developed naturally from a build-up of manure, or where hair and/or organic materials have been added to "improve" the footing.

Sands that lack stability or soil strength are a result of particles that are either round or in a narrow particle-size range, such as seventy to eighty percent of particles being in one size range. These sands feel soft and do not provide good traction.

There is nothing mystical about the term *holistic*. Basically, it involves interrelated cause-and-effect relationships. Studying these relationships allows you to select the right "tool" for treating a problem, whether it be dust, hardness, drainage, dead areas, or slick spots. Only when you know the cause can you make an accurate decision for treatment. Alternative solutions can range from using soil amendments to changing watering practices to using different equipment for working the arena.

ADDITIONAL COMMENTS

There are very few arena footings in the world that are composed solely of one type of material, at least for very long. Even a new, "pure" sand footing will start out with different size sand grains. These grains each function a little differently from one another when it comes to moisture retention, dust potential, and the tendency for compaction. As time goes on, this same arena will develop more of the fine-grained material and will have some added organic matter from the horses. After further use, the presence of silt and clay will be identified through testing. These changes have been brought about by subjecting the sand to abrasion through the use and maintenance of the arena. You will now have a footing that holds water somewhat longer, is more subject to compaction, and shows some signs of drainage limitations. Here is the cause-and-effect principle at work. Things don't "just happen."

13

Footing Amendments

THE WHAT AND WHY OF AMENDMENTS

With regard to equine arenas, an amendment is any material that is added to the footing for the purpose of improving the performance of the arena for the equine athlete. Amendments usually involve materials that can reduce the dust potential, hardness problems, and drainage difficulties and increase the option for a safe performance. Stephen G. Soule, V.M.D., rates poor footing as one of the key factors in creating torn suspensory ligaments.[1] He also adds, "Any horse, in any discipline, can tear a suspensory."

Once the "perfect" arena is constructed, the art of maintenance must be started and continued following use and, in the case of outdoor arenas, exposure to the elements. The impact that a one-thousand-pound animal can have on a sand or dirt footing in various events can impart considerable compression, compaction, and direct abrasion on any arena surface. For this reason, we are continually looking for the magic potion that will reduce potential problems so as to make the arena relatively maintenance-free.

The two natural mineral footings, sand and dirt, show a wide variation within even the same county, let alone different parts of the country. Sand is a geologic material and will vary widely based on its mineralogy and its mode of origin—glacial, water deposit, or man-made. The best approach to know what the characteristics are for a particular sand is to run a particle-size distribution analysis plus a sieve analysis on the sand. It is the dominant grain size or in some cases, a rather even distribu-

---

1. Soule, S G. "Beat the Odds on Suspensory Tears," *Practical Horseman*, XXIV(4) (April, 1996): 78. (As told by Elaine Pascoe.)

tion of grain sizes, that determines how this sand will perform.

Dirt footings are usually mixtures of more than one soil type. To test the suitability of this material, run an analysis of particle-size distribution and organic matter content. Interpretation can then be made regarding the soil's suitability and what amendment(s), if any, could improve its performance.

KNOW YOUR BASIC PROBLEM

If dryness is a problem which leads to dust, very likely your main objective is to improve the water retention of your footing. In this case, adding sand to a dirt arena is not the answer, since sand has very low water-holding properties. Rubber alone will help some, but rubber with nylon fiber still attached will help more.

If your arena is too wet, the addition of rubber will help, but you also need to look at your watering schedule. Are you watering too often? Perhaps your footing is too thin and overlies a very tight or firm base. Or your base may be concave,

Saving money on your arena footing by using a less desirable material may cost more in the long run through veterinary bills. Photo from How to Use Leg Wraps, Bandages and Boots, *by Sue A. Allen, with permission.*

essentially providing a reservoir, rather than the desired convex base, which drains the excess water away from the facility.

Hardness in arenas may be due to several reasons. The texture of the footing may have a high compaction potential. Sandy loam is one of several textures that will compact easily. Straight sand arenas, including a good grade of washed sand, will have a higher than desired reading for hardness if the footing is even slightly less than two inches thick. Over-watering of sands—older ones in particular—can result in "dead" or hard surfaces.

Make a map of your arena and locate the problem areas. This needn't be of Rand-McNally quality, but just a sketch locating the area and type of problem. This not only will be of value to you as a "to do" reminder, but also will help others who may be watering or dragging the arena when you are not there.

SOME SIMPLE TESTS

To test for hardness in dirt arenas, fill an empty soup or tuna can with moist footing, tamp the can two or three times by dropping the container onto a firm surface from a height of one or two inches, and set it in a sunny area or in your office where it can dry out. After the footing dries thoroughly, note if it sets up hard or remains quite friable. Any dirt footing that sets up as hard could use some organic matter and, possibly, some rubber.

A simple test to determine how fast your sand is breaking down under use is to compare a sample of new sand of the type you originally ordered with that of the footing material that has been used for six months or longer. This test is a simple process using Calgon water softener liquid. Use several one-quart jars. Place a half cup of *new, unused* sand in a quart jar. Fill the jar halfway with water, add two tablespoons of the liquid Calgon, and shake it vigorously for one minute. When you stop shaking, the water will have a cloudy appearance that will vary with the amount of silt, clay, and organic matter found in the sample. Seal this jar and keep it as a reference. Next take a sample of sand from several areas in the arena and repeat the process described above. The used sand will be cloudier and will take considerably longer to settle out if it has accumulated sufficient impurities. These impurities in the dry state represent your dust potential (see page 96).

This simple test demonstrates the relative amount of fines in your footing compared with the new or unused sand. The term fines *refers to very fine sand, silt, and clay, which tend to take longer to settle when in a water-Calgon mixture.*

CHECK YOUR MAINTENANCE

Watering

Is your watering all that it can be? Most commonly people tend to under-water, resulting in a moist surface "skin" (one-eighth to one-quarter inch deep) with dry soil immediately below. Under these conditions, you'll have a dust problem within a very short time after the traffic starts. Basically, proper watering involves applying water at a rate in which the water runs into the material instead of off it, and sufficient in amount and time to preclude dry subsurface layers. The frequency of watering will depend on the amount of silt, clay, and organic matter in the sand, the thickness of the footing, and the ambient humidity.

Dragging

- If you drag too infrequently, hardness can develop.
- If you drag too deeply, you lose the support of your base.
- If done when the surface is too wet, you invite clod formation on dirt arenas, necessitating extra passes to get rid of the clods.

Uniformity of Footing

Both the composition of the footing (texture) and the condition of the footing (related to water handling and soil strength) need to be examined. The term *water handling* relates to how well or poorly water enters the footing. An area that is slow to let the water penetrate not only provides a slick surface but also can have a dry sub-surface. Some footing materials provide a good grip and resist movement (within reason) and are called "high strength." Those materials which have too much give to them (poor soil strength) need to have an amendment that increases the soil strength. This can be important in a number of events, but is particularly important in jumping.

SOIL AMENDMENTS

When it comes to amendments, remember that there is no single recipe for success—one size does *not* fit all. The selection of an amendment depends on what you are starting with: type of footing, condition of your footing, type of use and events, and whether the arena is indoor or outdoor. With an amendment you also may need to change your watering procedure. An outdoor arena is usually less fine-tuned because of its being subject to the elements of nature. A moderate to high intensity rainfall can impart a significant amount of compaction even without any horse traffic. In many cases what your neighbor uses and is happy with may not work well for you at all; in some instances, it may. Assume nothing.

Types of Amendments

Both the number of products and the number of product representatives are growing. If any of these products comes across as "magic," curing all your ills, and seems too good to be true, it probably is. The bottom line is for you to know your arena better than most sales representatives. A sales representative must be able to tell you how the product will work *for your particular arena*. This is one of the most important points.

Materials most commonly sold as additives or amendments include rubber, polymers, and wood products (fiber, chips, sawdust, shavings). *Rubber* functions primarily to improve porosity, decrease the bulk density (weight per cubic foot), increase the cushion, reduce compaction, and improve drainage. It has a long life in the footing and, depending on the percentage of its concentration, can extend the life of sand footing by decreasing abrasion. *Polymers*' main purpose is to increase moisture retention. However, it is necessary to replace a polymer from time to time—a fairly expensive procedure. *Wood products* have some cushioning effect and are readily available and reasonably priced. On the downside, they can be slippery when wet and dusty when dry, and they break down and may have potential contaminants, depending on the source of the wood. For example, wood products previously treated with materials to retard rot are potentially hazardous.

Sand

One of the most common amendments used to correct problems in dirt arenas is sand. The process of adding a certain material to your footing is known as *blending*. Depending on the state of your footing problem, you may have to apply fifty percent or more of an amendment by volume to notice any improvement. If you are considering adding sand, the benefits that you are planning on can best be derived from the use of *washed* sand. Unwashed sand, while somewhat cheaper, often will compound the problem you already have by raising the silt and clay content of your surface.

Blending can be successful but only after all the unknowns are resolved. In all cases, make it a point to know what you are starting with through a lab analysis of your footing, with a particle-size analysis as a minimum. The same analysis could be helpful regarding the sand to be added. Another test for the added sand is a sieve analysis. Sands to be avoided are those dominated by fine and very fine sizes.

If you don't have easy access to a lab to run these tests or if your budget is limited, you can run a simple test yourself. This involves the use of two 1-gallon cans. Fill one can nearly full of your problem footing. Fill the second can with a blend of twenty-five percent sand, seventy-five percent footing and mix thoroughly. Add only enough water to the two cans until it runs out the bottoms. Manipulate both mixtures by hand. Note any differences between the two samples. After they dry out, check them again to see if the treated can is considerably looser. If no appreciable difference is observed, dump out the blend. This time, use fifty percent by volume of each of the sand and the footing, and repeat the tests, both moist and dry. Whatever blend you come up with using the gallon cans (let's say it is fifty percent sand by volume), when actually applying the sand to your arena, it would be smart to start out by adding only half of what appeared feasible from your testing (here, twenty-five percent). Additional sand can be added gradually, but if the fifty percent turns out to be too much in actual practice, it would be impossible to remove. In addition, you would have paid for sand that wasn't really needed.

Crumb Rubber

Rubber, or crumb rubber as it is frequently called, cannot perform well if it is applied to a surface material that has been degraded through excess wear and tear. A degraded sand is one that has an increase in the amount of "fines" in the sand (fine sand, very fine sand, and silt). These materials limit the effectiveness of the rubber.

Whether to mix the rubber into the surface sand or leave it on top can be a personal preference. Factors such as climate (humid vs. arid), and the type of event(s) can dictate how the rubber is positioned. Mixing the rubber into the surface will help to reduce abrasion between sand grains, thus decreasing dust.

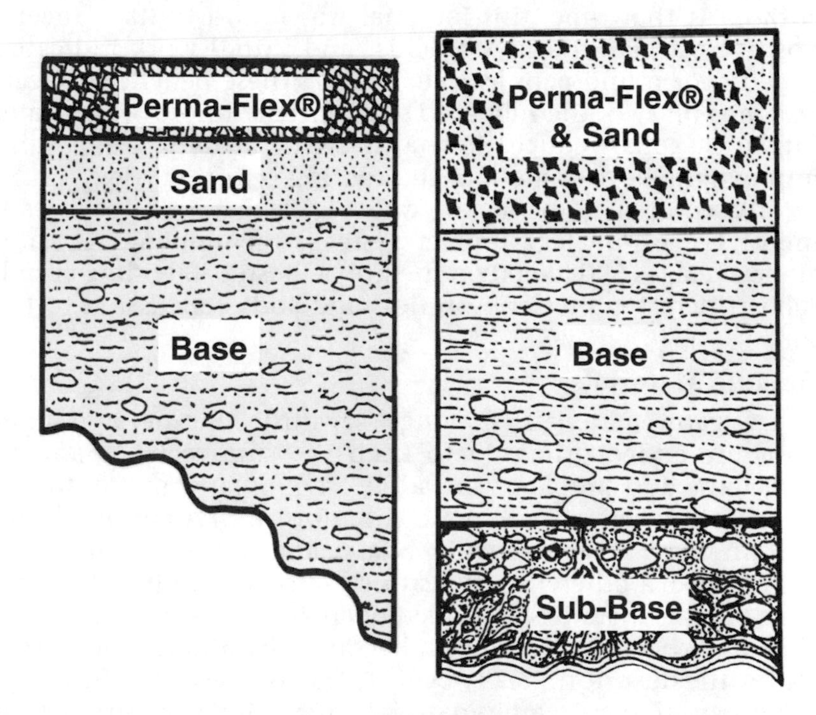

Left: Perma-Flex® High Performance Arena Footing added on the surface of the arena (1.5 inches of rubber over 1.5 inches angular sand). This application is recommended for jumping and dressage horses. Right: A blended combination of 1/3 Perma-Flex®, 2/3 sand, or two inches of Perma-Flex® on four inches of sand, is a good combination for any activity where the horse digs into the surface, such as barrel racing, team roping, cutting, team penning, and more.

This is a photo of Perma-Flex® High Performance Arena Footing, which is a manufactured crumb rubber product. Here it is used on top of the surface footing in the arena. Photo courtesy of Perma-Flex c/o American Rubber Technologies, Jacksonville, Florida.

The potential advantages of crumb rubber for use on equine facilities were identified in the early 1980s by the author. At that time, this material was found to have several positive effects on athletic fields, and initial work indicated benefits for round pens as well. Among these beneficial effects was the ability of the rubber to substantially improve the water intake of soils, reduce the hardness of athletic fields, and improve the development of the rooting of turf grasses.

Based upon some Japanese racing studies an impact reading of 125 on a Clegg Impact Tester is recommended. Sand alone averages 500 to 600 on the impact tester. Blending crumb rubber increases shock absorption and adds concussion to the soil.

Organic Materials

Organic materials (shavings, sawdust, manure, and compost) are added primarily to keep the surface loose and to reduce the dust problem. The addition of organic matter to any soil material tends to increase the moisture retention of that soil; however, this may require a large amount of organic material to make a difference. It also needs to be kept in mind that once organic materials are added to an arena, it should never be allowed to become dry. Once it becomes dry and is subjected to traffic, the dust storm really begins. This is a result of the breaking down of the organic material to smaller size particles, at which time it more easily becomes air-borne. Also remember that heavy application of organic material, especially manure, can result in slippery footing when moist. Manure applications are *not* recommended for reasons related to animal health.

Synthetic Materials

Synthetic materials have been used as amendments to improve the footing in arenas over the years. Most of these that I have seen do not increase the moisture retention of the footing but act more to keep the footing loose by "diluting" it. Polymer-coated sand has been used on at least one major race track with less than hoped-for results.

14

Manure Management

"No man is an island, entire of itself. . . ."
John Donne, 1624

THE PROBLEM

With the increased number of horse owners in the United States, the question arises as to how compatible their farms/ ranchettes are with urban areas. Odor and fly problems from the piles of manure have long been an issue. Dust from arenas soon followed, and now comes the challenge of water quality. The latest count of horses in the United States shows six million of these animals.

The Clean Water Act, which became effective in the 1970s, was passed to ensure safe drinking water. While there are a number of sources of water pollution, agriculture in general and livestock in particular have gained prominence in the public perception.

Cleaning out horse stalls entails having a place to put the manure. It could mean spreading it on your land, stockpiling it in hopes of finding a taker—which doesn't happen on a regular basis—or hauling it to a landfill, if you can find one that will accept it. These methods of handling manure can each have their shortcomings, whether it be problems with flies, odor, or groundwater pollution. Keep in mind that manure, while being a good source of nutrients for plant growth, needs to be applied with judgment. Fields can be rated for their ability to handle applications of manure. The potential for nutrient run-off from the manure will depend on proximity to water courses, slope, location in a flood plain, soil drainage and any seasonal concentrated flows of water. All in all, composting the manure certainly has some pluses.

The manure pile waiting to be dealt with.

CONVERTING A WASTE TO A RESOURCE

Composting is an age-old process involving the partial microbial decomposition of accumulated organic materials, resulting in the formation of humus, or compost. This aerobic process requires adequate levels of oxygen and moisture. The temperature of the stack needs to be monitored to determine the level of activity and the need for turning. Temperatures of 160°F should be maintained for three to five days to control the pathogens and weed seeds in the manure. Turning is essential to replenish the oxygen of the microbes if they are to do their job in a respectable time frame.

FACTORS IN SITE SELECTION

Composting is an excellent method of consolidating your manure into a beneficial material for the physical, chemical, and biological parameters of soils. Care must be taken in selecting a site for composting, however, since large quantities of manure will be concentrated on this site for several months, creating a potential for nutrient run-off and for the leaching of nutrients below ground. This potential is important when manure is stacked prior to composting as well as during the composting process itself.

The nutrients of concern are nitrogen and phosphorous. In order to minimize run-off, a safe distance between the operating site and water courses must be provided. Other significant factors are slope, location in the flood plain, soil drainage capabilities, and whether seasonally concentrated flows of water occur from run-off or melting snow. Soil depth and texture are also important. Due to their additional water-holding capacity, deep, loamy-textured soils are much preferred over shallow, sandy soils.

USES OF COMPOST

During the process of composting, manure will lose fifty to seventy percent of its volume. The range in shrinkage is due to the carbon-nitrogen ratio of the manure, the relative amount and type of bedding (straw, shavings, sawdust), and how near to optimum the environment of the stack (its temperature, moisture, and oxygen) was kept for the composting process.

The composting process requires three to six months. Shorter time frames are possible, but usually a period of maturing is necessary before the material is used. If the material is allowed to "mature" in the stack, earthworms will work it over, getting the material into even finer condition.

Specific uses for compost are:

- Top dressing for lawns.
- Soil modification during soil preparation of new or renovated facilities (e.g., athletic fields, golf courses, residential lawns, flower beds).
- A component for potting mixes.
- Top dressing on watershed areas to improve the chemical, physical, and biological parameters and ultimately to enhance water handling so as to reduce run-off.
- An addition to soil on degraded lands associated with mining activity to enhance the establishment of an effective vegetative cover.

ADDITIONAL COMMENTS

It is not uncommon to hear reports that horse manure is difficult to compost. This can be true where the manure has a high carbon content (shavings and straw being the most common culprits here), compared to the amount of animal waste.

This difficulty can be remedied by the addition of lawn clippings—alternate two- to three-inch layers with the manure, and thoroughly mix. If lawn clippings aren't available, a light application of a nitrogen fertilizer will be helpful to help break down the carbon material.

Whether we call it "manure management," "waste management," or "resource management" makes little difference. The bottom line is simply that we have to deal with manure. In addition to the leaching of nutrients into the groundwater from manure piles, the potential for harboring flies, other insects and disease are real concerns. As water quality and air quality receive increased attention, manure management will become an ever more important part of our equine facility.

15

Purchasing Land

Once you have decided that horses are to be a part of your life and that you prefer to keep them on a place of your own, your next step will be to see what is on the market in your area. Talking with friends and realtors plus reading the real estate section in the classified section of your paper will reveal what's on the market and the range in prices of available land. If the "sticker price" doesn't scare you away, you are ready for the next step, that of determining what land features you need as well as what things you should avoid.

THE LAUNDRY LIST

One of the most common tracts of land for sale today is the thirty-five-acre ranchette. The reasons for the thirty-five-acre figure are based, at least in part, on regulations regarding septic tanks, groundwater protection, and safe drinking water. With smaller parcels you and your neighbor could be sharing effluent unknowingly.

If you find yourself pressured by a salesperson to take one of the "last remaining" ranchettes, you need to take out your trusty check list and go over each point with him or her. Buying acreage for a horse facility requires some of the same items you would need to check if the tract were just a place to live away from the hustle and bustle of the city. This includes reasonable commuting distance, all utilities already in (or at least available), no serious limitations regarding the suitability for building sites, the quantity and quality of the water if a well is your only choice, and finally, esthetics.

When you are keeping horses, there are additional concerns over and above what have just been mentioned. These include the following:

Soil

The soil type is going to determine how suitable this material is for a natural arena with little or no materials brought in. Soils with a high clay content will be slow to dry out once they are wet, and will be subject to compaction more easily than sandy soils. Clayey soils will require more frequent working and will require more power to get them into a suitable condition.

Drainage

There are two considerations for drainage. One refers to streams that may be on the property; this is known as *surface drainage*. The other is *internal drainage* and refers to the relative ease or difficulty that water, whether rainfall, snow melt, or irrigation water, enters the soil and passes on down, allowing the surface soil to be drier and usable as a footing. Most properties traversed by a stream will bring an extra price. If you are considering property by a stream, check the probability of the stream reaching flood stage. Neighbors or the local Natural Resources Conservation Service office may be of help to you on this matter. Even a 100-year flood plain situation has no real comfort index. This term implies the land in question is not likely to be flooded more frequently than once in 100 years. However, this is man trying to outguess Mother Nature—often a losing proposition.

Climate/Weather

Climate pretty well tells you what you can expect regarding seasonal temperature ranges, precipitation, and humidity. Weather, on the other hand, is a combination of meteorological events, announced or unannounced, that can influence the events we had planned for the day. Such events can be rain, snow, wind, hail, tornadoes, fog, hurricanes, and unseasonable temperatures. These events can fit in with our plans, such as a light rain arriving in time so that we don't have to water the outdoor arena. The flip side, of course, is rain falling so heavily that the arena events have to be canceled. Excessive winds, as well as thunder and lightning, can also cancel outdoor events. While very few locations have perfect weather the year around, some areas are better than others. Abundant precipitation ("very adequate precipitation" may perhaps be a better term), on the other hand, can be a real plus for your pasture or hay growth. Again, timing is key, particularly with regard to hay.

While you have little control over weather or climate—with the exception of applying irrigation water if the dry season goes on too long—the point in this discussion is to alert you to the important role they can play in your geographical area. Soil and climate/weather are closely tied together because whether you are concerned with equine events in the arena or the ability to produce maximum hay and pasturage, together they can function well for what you plan to do with your land or, in some cases, they can reduce the effective use of your property.

Water

Water is key to all forms of life. Researchers tell us we can live longer without food than we can without water. Ideally, it should be available in the right place, at the right time, at the right price and of suitable quality.

Buying land out of the city limits should involve as many questions about the water as you ask about the soil and buildings. The key question concerning water is in regard to its source. If you are not on city water, this question becomes more important. Well water, in addition to water from springs, will need tests for quality as well as reliability throughout the year. Wells in areas where mining is active or has been active in the

Considerations you may want to think about are what events in your area are popular, and what your future interests may be for the events to be held in your arena. Friesian being ridden in a dressage test. Photo by Dusty Perin.

past should be tested for a number of metals which may be in concentrations that exceed the levels for safe drinking. In areas where septic tanks and wells coexist, tests should be run to be sure the effluent and groundwater have not intermingled. Arid and semiarid areas in particular, and on occasion any area which has periodic lower-than-normal precipitation, can give rise to short supplies of water, limiting the watering of your arena for dust control and providing inadequate amounts of drinking water for man and beast.

Everyone needs some time to call their own.

Slope and Aspect

Slope of land is commonly given in a percentage as the number of feet of slope in 100 feet. A two percent slope is a gentle slope; any slope less than this is of little or no concern for most uses. As the slope increases in steepness above two percent, problems increase with regard to erosion potential and different types of construction. Arenas, for example, are the cheapest to construct, other things being equal, on slopes of zero to one percent. As the slope increases, the need for cut-and-fill work also increases. This involves greater demands on equipment and time. Increased slope also means increased potential for run-off and erosion.

Aspect refers to the dominant direction the slope faces. South-facing slopes, for example, tend to be more droughty and require extra water for the establishment and growth of vegetation. The steeper the slope, the more pronounced the problem, since run-off is greater and less water has a chance to enter the soil for effective use by the plants. This necessitates the use of irrigation, if water is available, to obtain suitable growth. An arena constructed on a south slope will have a higher water requirement than one with a north aspect. The north-aspect slopes tend to be shielded from more of the sun's rays and consequently lose less moisture to evaporation.

WEATHER EXTREMES OR CLIMATE CHANGE?

At the writing of this handbook, an increasing number of climatologists have analyzed our wide variations in temperature and precipitation as being the results of global warming. Some, however, still maintain our weather has always been variable. Whatever the cause, our planet will continue to be subject to weather extremes. Those extremes in temperature and precipitation can have their impact on equine facilities, ranging from flooding to increased water demands in periods of drought to longer or shorter periods of frozen footing, particularly in outdoor arenas.

It is crucial when buying your horse facility to select acreage with the least tendency for being inundated by flooding. This not only includes those areas adjacent to streams that can be subject to overflowing but also soils which may have low water-holding capacity for a variety of reasons. Check that already existing facilities do not lie in low or concave sites which could become inundated during excessively high rainfall. The Fort Collins, Colorado flood in July of 1997 was partially due to an excessive rainfall in a short period of time, which created havoc for certain structures along Spring Creek. However, some parts of the city not near any body of water received damage. With their storm sewers flooded beyond capacity, the streets diverted water to lower lying areas, resulting in flooded buildings.

Some helpful information can be obtained from the soils map for your county, but frequently the scale of the mapping may not be of sufficient detail to identify those lands lying in subtle concave positions, which can put your facility at risk. Your best bet, short of hiring a drainage engineer, is to observe closely where the water seems to collect in light to moderate storms and then avoid using these sites for construction.

PLAN TO BE A GOOD NEIGHBOR

With a fixed amount of land on this planet and a population that continues to grow, neighbors will live closer than ever before. Without a doubt, horse farms will benefit by going the extra mile so finger-pointing can't get started. The "finger-pointing" I'm referring to implies complaints regarding odors, flies, dust, and pollution from drainage—all of the above from the manure pile. Avoid this problem from even beginning with a realistic program for manure management. This includes regular cleaning of stalls, and selecting a well-drained area for piling the manure until it can be spread on your fields, composted or someone located who will pick it up and use it on his or her farm. Finally, do all that you can to contain all water on your land following rain or during snow melt. Use effective control measures to minimize odor and dust on your facility.

ADDITIONAL COMMENTS

Getting what you want when purchasing land takes time. This includes time to collect the facts on a particular parcel, some of which may be apparent only at certain times of the year. One very good example is the question of an all-weather access road to the property. This can be important nearly anywhere, but it can be more of a concern in the mountainous western United States, where government land and private land may be interwoven.

In arid and semiarid lands, check out any irrigation canals on your property to be sure they are lined with concrete to minimize loss of water. It is not uncommon for canals to lose water sufficient to cause wet basements or saturated soils.

If your plan is to provide pasture or, possibly, raise some hay, check out the suitability of the land for this. The soil survey map for the county very often rates the soils for specific uses.

Even though your visit to the property may reveal nothing but open space, check with the County Planning Office to find out if there are any plans for development nearby that could cramp your style.

A considerable amount of technical information is available to help you select your land as well as capitalize on its use and management. Three such sources are:

- Soil Survey Report (for your county)
- Climatological Data
- County Agricultural Extension Service

Table 7.
Potential Site Problems in Selecting an Equine Facility.

PROBLEM	POSSIBLE CAUSES	DEALING WITH THE PROBLEM
Excess wetness	Tight soil, drain tile plugged, run-off/run-on	Soil modification, clean out tile, terracing, ditching.
Wind	Nature	Windbreaks
Water shortage	Questionable supply, excess use of water, inherent soil problems (droughty, poor penetration)	Water only as needed, in evening, water harvesting.[1]
Soil	Droughty, drainage, cracking clays	Soil modification, adding of organic matter; install drainage—can be a costly problem, Avoid![2]
Hazardous waste, mine wastes	Landfill, mining activity	Avoid! Hazards range , from pollution of ground water to toxic plants, live-stock and humans subject to radiation exposure.
Odor, flies	Accumulation of manure	Regular cleaning of stalls; use of suitable bedding. Dispose of manure by spreading on land or arrange for composting.
Groundwater pollution	On-site "dump"	Make certain that your on-site landfill is run as a landfill and not a "dump."

1. Water harvesting is the capturing of the precipitation from a catchment area such as a roof or a treated hillside and using it for irrigation or for arena watering. This water may be either stored for later use or applied directly.

2. These soils are also known as vertisols or self-mulching soils. The State of Colorado has a considerable acreage of these soils and litigation measures are not uncommon between the developer/builder and the buyer with regard to building damages where adequate foundation was not designed. This group of soils would also pose a problem where they are used as a base or sub-base for equine arenas.

Glossary

Abrasion: The wearing down of particles resulting from the rubbing together of two particles. Sand grains become more rounded due to the weight of the horse on the sand footing.

Aerification: The "opening up" of a tight soil through the use of a coring machine which permits better drainage and the movement of oxygen to the roots of turf plants.

Amendment: Any dissimilar material mixed with a footing material to modify the footing in hopes of improving its performance. Examples might be organic materials, crumb rubber, or sand to reduce the tendency for compaction and improve water handling.

Atterberg Limits: A laboratory test representing the moisture contents at which the soil changes behavior. One example is the identification of those soils with a high affinity for water with a greater tendency for swelling and clod development. Soils in this category can be problematic for arenas.

Base: The base lies between the footing and the sub-base on the arena floor. The function of the base is to provide a uniform support throughout the arena.

Chinook Wind: A warm, dry wind that descends the eastern slopes of the Rocky Mountains. This wind may not be readily discernible but its ability to melt snowdrifts is well known.

Clay: A soil particle so small that it cannot be seen with the naked eye. Most soils contain sand, silt, and clay. When the clay content is significantly high, clod formation is common and drainage problems may occur.

Clay Mineralogy: Different types of clays often exhibit some very different characteristics, affecting the use and management of the soil material in which it is found. Kaolinite and montmorillonite (bentonite) are two clay types.

Clegg Impact Tester: This device, developed by Dr. B. Clegg, an Australian engineer, provides an objective measurement (called a *Clegg Impact Value* (*CIV*)) of soil firmness or impact absorption characteristics.

Clods/Cloddy: Certain soils have a tendency to form oval or nearly round "balls" on the surface. To break them up requires additional working of the arena when the soil is dry. Cloddiness implies a certain amount of silt and clay is present.

Compaction: Soil compaction results when pressures on the soil exceed the bearing capacity. The risk of excessive compaction increases as the wheel landing increases, the draft increases, the tire pressure increases, and the number of passes increases. Compacted soil has a higher injury potential to horse and rider than a non-compacted surface.

Compost: Material formed by the action of friendly microorganisms (bacteria, fungi, etc.) on breaking down raw organic material over a period of time (three to six months) when conditions of temperature, moisture and oxygen levels are ideal. The end product has an earthy odor and looks similar to peat.

Condition: A term referring to the degree of "readiness" of an arena. Suitable condition implies little, if any, dust problem and that an arena is free of excessive hardness that it is not slippery, and that it has a suitable holding power, depending on the event.

Consistence: Refers to the uniformity of the footing as well as the base. One example for the footing is a uniform thickness over the base. The base should be relatively free of soft spots, ridges, and "holes."

Crumb Rubber: Refers to rubber within a stated diameter range, most frequently derived from old tires that have been shredded with the metal removed and with or without varying amounts of nylon fiber. One of the most common sizes used for equine arenas is the 1/4-3/8" range in diameter.

Degradation: The loss or weakening of a physical, chemical, or biological component of a material which in turn reduces its function(s) compared to new material. One example with arena footings is the lack of resiliency of sand after the sand grains have been worn down through abrasion.

Diversion Ditch: A ditch of variable size running across the dominant slope at a particular grade to intercept run-off and dispose of it before it can cause erosion and possibly flooding.

Drainage: This term can be used to describe how well water may move down through the soil so as not to create a wetness problem. It also has reference to the lateral movement of water across an arena which was designed with a particular slope on top of a prepared base to a drain pipe. Without adequate drainage, an outdoor arena can remain too wet for use for a number of days.

Dust: Dust is the by-product when abrasion starts to work on the materials of most footings. Dust particles can be comprised of sand, silt, clay, and organic matter. Since silt and clay are, by definition, of smaller diameters than sand, they travel the farthest and require less of a force to move them compared to sand.

Dust Potential: Certain materials are much more prone to dust formation when arenas are in use. Footings with a high silt content or other materials which do not absorb moisture well or do not retain moisture very long after it is absorbed are just a few examples.

Effluent: Refers to the liquid waste coming from human sewage or from manure that has been subjected to snow and rain accumulation. This liquid product with its accumulation of salts, including nitrates, may then infiltrate the groundwater where it becomes labeled as a pollutant.

Footing: The surface material for an arena on which the equine athlete is expected to perform his or her best. A user-friendly footing is relatively dust- and odor-free and resilient and will require a maintenance program keyed to your particular use and environment.

Footing Enhancer: Any material added to the footing to improve its performance and/or maintenance. Examples are sand, rubber, and wood shavings. Enhancers can vary depending upon the particular need in a specific geographical area.

Gravel: Mineral material which may be found occurring naturally in soils. It is larger than sand (over 2.0 mm) and can be up to 3.0 inches in its longest dimension. Angular gravel should be removed from dirt arenas because of the potential damage to the hoof.

Hardness: The hardness of an arena or racecourse can vary with the type of material, moisture content and the type and frequency of use. The Clegg Impact Soil Tester is commonly used to monitor soil firmness. This device provides an objective measurement (called a *Clegg Impact Value* (*CIV*)) of soil firmness or impact absorption characteristics.

Heaving: Heaving, causing an upward movement of large gravel and stones, is caused by frost action in the soils. It is more common in some soils than others and is most prevalent when a soil is moist rather than dry.

Holistic: An approach that recognizes that the interaction of the various parts of a material and their condition largely determines the performance of that material and likewise will dictate the management requirements to achieve optimum performance.

Hydrophobic: Refers to any water-repellent material or condition. Heavy accumulation of organic matter and contrasting layers of mineral soil may create hydrophobic conditions.

Man-Made Soils: In contrast to naturally-occurring soils or those soils formed in place, man-made soils have had soil material added to a site. One example is the addition of "fill" material to an arena, football field or soccer field. When this is done without a good match of the materials brought in to those already present, the results may be disastrous.

Mantle: Earth's surface—the soil material overlying bedrock or other firm, in-place material. The mantle can range in thickness from a few inches to tens of feet. This material is the source for dirt arenas and athletic fields as well as for crop production.

Mechanical Analysis: Determines particle-size distribution, that is, the various amounts of the different soil separates (sand, silt, and clay) in a soil sample. These percentages are then used to determine soil texture (e.g., sandy loam, silty clay).

Mineral Matter: Broadly defined, this is the inorganic portion of a substance. In soils, the organic portion may be from one to four percent with the remainder comprised of separate minerals such as quartz and calcium or combinations of minerals in the form of rock types—granite and basalt.

Mineralogy: The study of individual minerals. In dirt facilities, *clay mineralogy* is the identification of particular types of clay, such as montmorillonite/illite and gibbsite, which can affect the performance of the facility.

Organic Matter: Refers to the dark material common to the surface layer of most soils. It consists of organic materials of plant and animal origin that have been acted upon by microorganisms in the soil. Little evidence remains of what the material was originally derived from.

Organic Material: Refers to those materials of plant origin. Organic material is an important component for the composting process as described in the chapter on manure. It is also an important consideration as an additive to improve certain footing problems. Examples are compost, sawdust, shavings, straw, and manure.

Particle-Size Distribution (PSD): See *Mechanical Analysis*.

Percent Slope: The number of feet, or fractions thereof, that a land surface slopes in 100 feet of distance. For arenas, a one to two percent slope may be needed to remove excess water from a facility. This becomes more critical for outdoor arenas where water amounts from precipitation are unpredictable.

Performance: This characteristic of an arena is based upon its response to: 1) *environmental conditions* (snow, wind, rain, temperature, and humidity); 2) *working the arena* (the effect of specific equipment on the footing and water handling); and 3) *the degree of suitability* for a particular type of event.

Polymers: Synthetic products (one of which is known technically as hydrophilic polyacrylamide gel) marketed as amendments to increase the water-holding capacity of arena footings, having as well a number of horticultural applications.

Pore Space/Porosity: The degree to which the total volume of a soil is permeated with pores. The smaller pores hold water and the larger pores carry oxygen and carbon dioxide. The more porous a soil, the more friable it is.

Resiliency: Surfaces of equine facilities (arenas and racecourses) as well as athletic facilities have a degree of firmness which may be acceptable or unacceptable for the safe use by the equine or human athlete. The deceleration peak measured by a Clegg Impact Tester (see *Clegg Impact Tester*) is the basis for establishing a safe resiliency or impact absorption.

Rhizomes: Horizontal underground stems usually sending out roots and above-ground shoots at the nodes.

Ridging: With reference to the arena base, a situation where tillage equipment such as a disc harrow has been used and has inadvertently created a pattern of miniature ridges and valleys in the surface of the base. Most often this goes unnoticed, but the impact on the horse can be serious.

Run-Off: Moisture in the form of snow or rain that is in excess of the soil's absorption capability, resulting in the excess running off the surface, potentially causing erosion.

Run-On: An area subject to receiving run-off water from a surface lying up-slope. Areas that could receive run-on water should be avoided for construction unless special precautions are taken, including diversions, fill, etc.

Sand: A soil separate ranging from 2.0 mm to 0.05 mm in size. Sand purchased for an arena footing should be dominated by medium to fine sand with some coarse and very little very fine sand. The amount of sand in a sample is determined by the particle-size distribution analysis.

Sand Hardness: Sand grains vary in hardness based mainly on the mineralogy of the sand and, to some extent, its mode of origin. Quartz sand is the hardest; beach sand dominated by calcium carbonate from coral and shells is softer.

Shape (of Sand Grains): This is best determined by a ten- or twenty-power hand magnifier. Some grains will be seen to be round, others angular, and some a combination of shapes. Round sands are commonly the result of wave action in rivers and oceans.

Side-Cast Material: Refers to the "throwing" of material to either side of the horse. There will be a noticeable accumulation along the rail, with somewhat heavier amounts on the turns.

Silt: A soil separate with a diameter ranging from 0.05 to 0.002 mm. The amount of silt in a sample is determined by the particle-size distribution analysis.

Soil Aggregates: A group of primary soil particles (sand, silt and clay) that cohere to each other more strongly than to other surrounding particles. This is also known as *soil structure*. Well-developed aggregates are key to good turf growth and good soil drainage.

Soil Structure: See *Soil Aggregates*.

Soil Survey Report: A report for most counties in the United States describing the soils for that county and their classification for different uses. This is put out by the National Cooperative Soil Survey, Washington, D.C.

Soil Strength: In general, this term describes the "grip" or "holding power" of a particular soil. It is very important to assess in Western riding, particularly in barrel racing and cutting horse events.

Soil Type: A term for describing soils that are alike in all characteristics including the texture of the topsoil (called the *A-horizon* on soil maps). This unit of soil classification is found in the county Soil Survey Report.

Sprig: A section of grass stems cut into pieces several inches long. When these sprigs are covered with a thin layer of soil, they will germinate and form a cover of grass for an outdoor arena, pasture, or athletic field.

Stolon: A horizontal stem which grows along the surface of the soil, sending out roots at the nodes.

Subsoil: Refers to that part of a soil below the surface soil. The subsoil may contain more clay and be quite firm. It is less fertile than the surface soil and roots may be concentrated in the surface soil for these reasons.

Texture: The relative proportions of sand, silt, and clay in a soil sample. Texture (loamy sand, sandy loam, loam, silty clay, for example) has a strong influence on the suitability of that soil for footing, base, and the growth of turf.

Topsoil: The layer of soil tilled in cultivation. It is quite often more fertile than the subsoil lying beneath it. Topsoil ranges from less than one inch to six to eight inches in thickness.

Traction: The ability to hold when a certain pressure is applied. This can refer to the pressure applied by power equipment, a human athlete or the equine athlete. Poor traction can create injuries. In the case of football, severe injuries of the knee have been identified with excessive traction between the playing surface and the shoe outsole.

Water Handling: The ability of a footing material as well as a base to accept water applications (rainfall or sprinklers) within an acceptable range without deteriorating and at the same time provide a safe, well-performing footing for the event.

Water-Holding Capacity: Every soil has a limit in its ability to absorb water. If water is applied above this amount, the excess water runs off and/or evaporates. Applying water in excess of the water-holding capacity is wasteful and sacrifices arena condition and safety.

Water Repellent: Certain soils have very little water-absorption capability. When this condition is present, the water tends to "bead" on the soil surface, with little if any entering the soil. The result in arenas is a constant dust problem. On turf arenas, it creates stress areas that remain brown.

Working the Arena: Refers to the use of different types of tools, usually tractor drawn, that can loosen up materials, even them out for uniform thickness, and break up clods, frequently concentrating on particular problem areas in the arena.

Bibliography

Arizona Department of Environmental Quality. *Consumers' Guide to Dust Control Technologies*, Office of Air Quality, June 1989, Phoenix, Arizona.

Cheney, J. A., Shen, C. K., Wheat, J. D. "Relationship of racetrack surface to lameness in the Thoroughbred racehorse," *American Journal of Veterinary Research* 34 (10) (1973): 1285-1289.

Hill, T., Maylin, G., Krook, L. "Track condition and racing injuries in Thoroughbred horses," *Cornell Veterinarian* 76 (1986): 361-379.

Malmgren, R. *The Land Buyer's Handbook*. Privately published. Fort Collins, Colorado.

Malmgren, R., Shideler, R.K., Butler, K.D. and Anderson, E.W. "The effect of polymer and rubber particles on arena soil characteristics," *Journal of Equine Veterinary Science* (14) January 1994.

Moyer, W., Spencer, P. A., Kallish, M. "Relative incidence of dorsal metacarpal disease in young Thoroughbred racing horses training on two surfaces." *Equine Veterinary Journal*, 23 (3) (1990): 166-168.

Sellnow, L. "The science of safety," *Blood-Horse,* September 1991: 4318-4320.

Smith, F. *History of Veterinary Medicine*, London: Ballieve-Tindall, 1919.

Soule, S. G. "Beat the Odds on Suspensory Tears," *Practical Horseman* XXIV (4) (April 1996): 78. (As told by Elaine Pascoe.)

U.S.D.A. "Soil Taxonomy, a Basic System of Soil Classification for Making and Interpreting Soil Surveys," Agricultural Handbook, No. 436 (1975).

Wight, B. *Windbreak For Rural Living*, Soil Conservation Services, James R. Brandle, University of Nebraska.

Zebarth, B. J., Sheard, R. W. "Impact and shear resistance of turf grass racing surfaces for Thoroughbreds," *American Journal of Veterinary Research* 46 (4) (1985): 778-786.

Reference Sources

MATERIALS

Crumb Rubber Products:
American Rubber Technology
(PERMA-FLEX)
P.O. Box 6548
Jacksonville, FL 32236-6548
(800) 741-5201

Sand & Gravel
Western Mobile/Lafarge
1800 N. Taft Hill Road
Ft. Collins, CO 80521
(970) 407-3750 - Ft. Collins, CO
(303) 657-4242 - Denver, CO

Water
Office of Arid Lands Studies
College of Agriculture
University of Arizona
845 N. Park Avenue
Tucson, AZ 85719

EQUIPMENT

Arena Groomer c/o PARMA Co.
P.O. Box 190
101 Main Street
Parma, ID 83660
(208) 722-5116
(208) 722-6012 - Fax

Arena Werks
Snodgrass Equipment
Joshua, TX 76058
(800) 644-3724
(817) 645-0590 - Fax

About the Author

Bob Malmgren graduated in 1950 from the University of Wisconsin as a Soil Scientist. He worked in Soil Mapping and Classification in Wisconsin, Washington, Hawaii, Montana, and Colorado with the U.S.D.A. Soil Conservation Service and the United States Forest Service from 1950 to1979. He traveled in eleven countries in Africa, Central and South America, Europe, and Asia studying soil-plant-water relationships and soil compaction.

Malmgren worked on a soil evaluation study on the Colorado State University hazardous waste site, and performed soil investigations on a proposed extension of the Larimer County Landfill (Colorado) in 1985 and 1993, respectively. He was granted two patents on the use of crumb rubber (equine footing) as an amendment for use on dirt arenas and turf facilities. From 1985 to 1990, he worked as a soils consultant on equine arenas, golf courses and athletic fields. Malmgren carried out investigations on the use and management of arena facilities and their relationship to hardness and dust problems at the Colorado State University facilities from 1991 through 1997.

Index